Good Housekeeping

Christmas Cookies!

Chocolate Chunk Cookies (recipe page 19)

Good Housekeeping

Christmas Cookies!

65 Recipes for Classic & New Holiday Treats

HEARST BOOKS

New York

HEARST BOOKS
New York

An Imprint of Sterling Publishing
387 Park Avenue South
New York, NY 10016

Good Housekeeping
Rosemary Ellis   Editor in Chief
Susan Westmoreland   Food Director
Samantha B. Cassetty, M.S., R.D.   Nutrition Director
Sharon Franke   Kitchen Appliances & Technology Director

Edited by Pam Hoenig
Production editor Sarah Scheffel
Book design by Laura Palese
Photography credits on page 127

KOHL'S
ISBN 978-1-61837-069-3
Factory Number: 123386
07/12

10 9 8 7 6 5 4 3 2 1

This special edition was printed for Kohl's Department Stores, Inc. (for distribution on behalf of Kohl's Cares, LLC, its wholly owned subsidiary) by Hearst Books, a division of Sterling Publishing Co., Inc.

Distributed in Canada by Sterling Publishing
c/o Canadian Manda Group, 165 Dufferin Street
Toronto, Ontario, Canada M6K 3H6

Distributed in Australia by Capricorn Link (Australia) Pty. Ltd.
P.O. Box 704, Windsor, NSW 2756 Australia

Manufactured in China

Sterling ISBN 978-1-61837-069-3

Contents

Happiness Is a Christmas Cookie 7

Bake the Best Cookies Ever! 8

Drop Cookies   17

Shaped Cookies   51

Icebox Cookies   81

Brownies & Bar Cookies   99

Metric Equivalents 122

Index 124

Photography Credits 127

Recipe Cards for You to Share 128

Chocolate Chip Cookies (recipe page 21)

Happiness Is a Christmas Cookie

Christmas is the perfect time for mixing up a few batches of cookies. So many of us have memories of jars, tins, and plates full of delicious treats during the holiday season. I happily recall our household serving up everyday cookies—chocolate chip, hermit, oatmeal-raisin, peanut butter, and biscotti—as well as special offerings for the season, like ginger cookies, macaroons, walnut balls, and cherry linzer bars.

Why buy pricey commercial cookies made with ingredients like palm oil, hydrogenated shortening, high-fructose corn syrup, and preservatives for "freshness" when baking your own homemade cookies is so simple? Cookies are truly one of the easiest baked goods to make, and they're a great way to create special holiday memories with children.

In *Christmas Cookies!*, we provide you with 65 scrumptious recipes for drop, shaped, icebox, and bar cookies that will delight your friends and family. These cookies are sturdy enough to stand up to being in a big cookie pile-up without crumbling or smooshing. They are perfect for traveling to a party or family gathering, and we include tips for packaging and mailing to distant friends and relatives. You'll find lots of nutty, chocolatey, crispy classics, as well as a few fun new creations, from Chipperdoodles to Caramel-Nut Brownies. Blank recipe cards in the back of the book allow you to share your favorites.

Let's bake!

Susan Westmoreland
Food Director, *Good Housekeeping*

Bake the Best Cookies Ever!

The good news is that cookies are easy to mix and bake. But because they are so simple, success is dependent on using good-quality ingredients and the right kind of equipment, as well as observing some basic rules when measuring, mixing, baking, and cooling.

It Starts with the Right Ingredients

To ensure that your cookies taste delicious and have just the right texture, it is important to use the exact ingredients called for in the recipe and to handle them properly.

- **Butter vs. margarine.** When a recipe calls for butter or margarine, we prefer salted butter. Do not substitute margarine for butter if a recipe does not give it as an option. For those recipes that do, if you prefer to use margarine, make sure it contains 80 percent fat. Don't substitute light margarine or vegetable-oil spreads for stick margarine, and don't use whipped butter, either. Those products contain more water or air than standard sticks and won't work in cookies unless the recipes have been formulated especially for them.

  To soften butter or margarine, let it stand, wrapped on a counter or unwrapped in a mixing bowl, at room temperature for an hour. You can speed up the process by cutting it into small pieces first. It's best not to soften butter or margarine in the microwave. The microwave may melt some areas, which can detract from the cookies' intended texture.

- **The type of flour is important.** Most cookie recipes call for all-purpose flour. Occasionally, a cookie recipe will call for cake flour, which is higher in starch and will produce a more tender cookie. Cake and all-purpose flours are not interchangeable, so read your recipe carefully. In either case, make sure the flour you are using is *not* self-rising.

- **White whole-wheat flour** is another option, especially if you're struggling to eat the recommended three servings of whole grains a day. It is sold by King Arthur Flour, among other brands. Milled from an albino variety of wheat, it's as healthy as traditional whole wheat, but lacks the heartier taste and grainy heft. It can be substituted for up to half of the all-purpose flour in many recipes, including sugar cookies or chocolate chip cookies, without substantially changing the taste.

- **Baking soda vs. baking powder.** Both products are leavening agents—they make cookies rise. Baking powder is a premeasured mixture of baking soda and an acid. Do not substitute baking soda for baking powder or vice versa. (It takes twice as much baking powder as baking soda to leaven a product.) Keep both products tightly closed in the box or tin they came in, stored in a cool, dry place so they stay active. For best results, replace baking soda and baking powder after six months if you haven't used them up.

  To test whether baking soda is still active, stir a teaspoonful into a cup containing a little white vinegar; if it froths up immediately and vigorously, it's active.

  To test whether baking powder is still active, stir a teaspoonful into a cup of hot tap water. If the water bubbles vigorously, it's as good as fresh. In the case of both baking soda and powder, delayed, little, or no bubbling means the leavener is past its prime.

  To measure baking soda or baking powder, use a clean, dry measuring spoon and level it off with a spatula or knife.

Know Your Chocolate and Cocoa

This collection includes a lot of recipes using chocolate and cocoa (yum!) in many different forms. You don't have to blow your budget by buying a super-premium brand, but don't skimp on quality either. Always use the type and amount of chocolate or cocoa specified in the recipe. Here's a guide to the types you'll find in our recipes:

- **Cocoa powder.** There are two types of unsweetened cocoa, alkalized (Dutch-processed) cocoa and nonalkalized (natural) cocoa. Dutch-processed cocoa is treated with an alkali to neutralize its acidity, which creates a darker but less intensely flavored cocoa. We use natural cocoa in our recipes. Look closely at the label when buying cocoa; some are alkalized even if the label doesn't use the term "Dutch-processed." Do not substitute instant cocoa mix for unsweetened cocoa.

- **Unsweetened chocolate.** Ground cocoa beans (called chocolate liquor) in solid form with no sugar added. It's sold in packages of 1-ounce squares, (3 to 3½ ounce) bars, or in bulk.

- **Bittersweet chocolate.** Chocolate that has been sweetened. The higher the level of chocolate liquor it contains, the less sweet it will be. Available in bars, packages of 1-ounce squares, chips, and bulk.

- **Semisweet chocolate.** This type of chocolate contains more sugar than bittersweet chocolate. It is available in bars, packages of 1-ounce squares, chips, and bulk.

- **Sweet chocolate.** A bakers' product that's sweeter than semisweet chocolate sold under the name German's Sweet Chocolate. Available in packages of 1-ounce squares and bars.

- **Chocolate chips.** Available in milk, semisweet, and bittersweet chocolate varieties and in mini, standard, or chocolate chunk shapes, what would cookies be without them? Today, you'll also find white chocolate, butterscotch, mint, and other whimsical flavors in stores, especially during the holidays.
- **White chocolate.** Chocolate in name only (it contains no chocolate liquor), white chocolate is vanilla-flavored sweetened cocoa butter (a byproduct of chocolate processing), although some brands substitute vegetable oil for the cocoa butter. For the best quality, choose a brand that contains cocoa butter.

  Melting chocolate: All types of chocolate should be melted in a double boiler over low heat to prevent scorching. Or place the chocolate in a microwave-safe bowl and microwave at 50 percent power, stirring at intervals. To speed melting, chop it into small pieces.

  Storing chocolate: Store chocolate, well wrapped, in a cool, dark place (65°F is ideal). If storage conditions are too cold, chocolate will "sweat" when brought to room temperature. If conditions are too warm, the cocoa will start to melt and a gray "bloom" will form on the surface. This doesn't affect the flavor of the chocolate.

Measuring Up

To get the same results every time you make a recipe, it is important to use standard measuring equipment and to measure carefully.

- **Measuring spoons.** Always use standard measuring spoons to measure both liquid and dry ingredients. For convenience, measure the dry ingredients first.
- **Measuring cups.** Use stackable dry ingredient cups with flat tops to measure dry ingredients; clear cups with spouts for liquids. Never use dry-ingredient cups to measure liquid ingredients or liquid-ingredient cups to measure dry ingredients.

Here are tips on measuring a variety of common cookie ingredients. To avoid waste, always measure ingredients over waxed paper or into an empty bowl but never over your bowl of already measured ingredients— just in case there is a spill.

- **Liquids.** Use a clear measuring cup with a spout. Place the cup on a level surface and bend down so that your eyes are in line with the marks on the cup.
- **Flour.** To measure flour, which tends to pack down in its storage container, stir and then spoon it into a standard-sized dry-ingredient measuring cup. Level the top surface with a spatula or back of a knife, scraping off the excess into a bowl.
- **Sugar.** Just scoop or pour *granulated sugar* into a dry-ingredient measuring cup, then level with the back of a knife. *Confectioners' sugar* should be sifted before measuring to break up clumps. Lightly spoon it into the measuring cup and then level. To measure *brown sugar*, pack it into the measuring cup and then level.
- **Butter and margarine.** Tablespoons are marked on the wrapper, so you can just cut off the desired amount using a knife.
- **Maple syrup, honey, and other sticky ingredients.** Lightly oil the liquid-ingredient measuring cup first, and the ingredient will pour right out without sticking to it.
- **Dough.** For best results, make all cookies the same size. If you bake a lot, invest in a cookie scoop with a trigger handle.

Mixing It Up

While a lot of cookie batters can be stirred up with whatever spoon is on hand, the right equipment makes this task easier. You should have:

- a stand mixer or hand beater
- a food processor or mini processor
- a set of mixing bowls: small, medium, and large
- several wooden spoons

Overmixing the dough results in tough cookies. Unless a recipe says otherwise, mix the dough just until blended after adding the flour.

Use the Right Cookie Sheet

High-quality cookie sheets and baking pans are a key component in cookie baking. You should use heavy-gauge metal sheets and pans with a dull finish—we recommend aluminum. These double-thick insulated cookie sheets and baking pans will help prevent your cookies from getting extra-dark bottoms. Avoid dark cookie sheets—they also can blacken the bottoms of cookies because they absorb more heat. If your cookie sheets are old and discolored, you can line them with foil to help deflect the heat.

Size is important. Cookie sheets should be at least 2 inches smaller in length and width than your oven so that air can circulate freely around them. So measure your oven before you buy new cookie sheets. If possible, buy rimless sheets, or those with only one or two edges turned. They allow more air to circulate around the cookies.

- **Greasing cookie sheets.** Your best bet is vegetable shortening. Avoid butter, which browns, and vegetable oil, which leaves a gummy residue on baking pans. Grease cookie sheets only when a recipe directs you to. Some cookies have a high fat content, so greasing isn't necessary.
- **Washing cookie sheets.** Wash them by hand, then place them in the oven (turned off but still warm from baking) to dry. This will keep them from rusting.

Get the Timing Right

You don't want to either underbake or overbake your cookies. Since cookies often bake at a high temperature for a short period of time, it's important to have an accurate gauge of your oven's temperature. If there is any question as to whether your oven is properly calibrated, buy a good oven thermometer. Then be sure your oven has fully preheated before you put a batch of cookies in. Start checking their doneness a couple of minutes early. A kitchen timer is a good investment. It's easy to get distracted, and just a few minutes can mean the difference between golden and burnt cookies.

The Importance of Cooling Properly

Once your cookies are done, set the sheet on a wire rack to cool (each recipe will tell you for how long). Then use a wide metal spatula to transfer the cookies to the racks to cool completely. This will prevent the cookies from overbaking and allow the bottoms to crisp properly. Once they are properly cooled, it's time for the cookie jar!

Drop Cookies

Nothing could be easier than baking up a batch of drop cookies. Whip together your cookie dough (which can be a simple sugar dough or elevated to sweet and crunchy heights with any number of add-ins, including dried fruit, white and dark chocolate chunks, coconut, and nuts of all sorts) and then use a teaspoon or tablespoon to transfer it to the cookie sheet. Fifteen minutes or less in the oven, and you've got Christmas cookie nirvana! Don't have time to bake all the dough? Cover it and refrigerate up to two days.

Cranberry-Chocolate Chunk Cookies (recipe page 40)

Here are a few tips for drop cookie success every time:

For even baking, try to scoop the same amount of dough for each cookie. When we say "Drop by rounded teaspoons" or "Drop by rounded tablespoons," we mean a measuring teaspoon or tablespoon, not a spoon to stir tea or a soupspoon.

For perfectly shaped cookies, be sure to leave the directed amount of space around each piece of dough on the cookie sheet; otherwise, the cookies may run into one another as the dough spreads in the hot oven, smooshing their edges together.

To keep the dough from spreading more than it should, be sure to drop the dough onto completely cooled cookie sheets. You don't want the dough to be exposed to any heat until it enters the oven.

If baking two sheets of cookies at a time, rotate the sheets between the upper and lower oven racks about halfway through the baking time to ensure even baking.

To keep cookies from sticking to the cookie sheet, always check greased sheets to see if they need regreasing between batches.

Chocolate Chunk Cookies

A holiday cookie jar just isn't well stocked unless there's something chocolate in it. This cookie is perfect for people who like a dose of decadence in their holiday treat.

active time 30 minutes *bake time* 10 to 11 minutes per batch *makes* 36 cookies

2½ cups all-purpose flour
1 teaspoon baking soda
½ teaspoon salt
1 cup butter or margarine (2 sticks), softened
1 cup packed brown sugar
½ cup granulated sugar
2 teaspoons vanilla extract
2 large eggs
8 squares (8 ounces) bittersweet chocolate, cut into ½-inch chunks
1 cup walnuts (4 ounces), coarsely chopped

1 Preheat oven to 375°F. Grease large cookie sheet.

2 In medium bowl, combine flour, baking soda, and salt.

3 In large bowl, with mixer on medium speed, beat butter and sugars until creamy, occasionally scraping bowl with rubber spatula. Beat in vanilla, then eggs, one at a time, beating well after each addition. On low speed, gradually add flour mixture; beat just until blended, occasionally scraping bowl. With wooden spoon, stir in chocolate and walnuts.

4 Drop dough by heaping measuring tablespoons, 2 inches apart, on prepared cookie sheet. Flatten with a small metal spatula as shown on page 45. Bake until lightly browned, 10 to 11 minutes. With wide metal spatula, transfer cookies to wire rack to cool. Repeat with remaining dough.

5 Store cookies in cookie jar up to 1 week.

each cookie About 170 calories, 3g protein, 19g carbohydrate, 10g total fat (5g saturated), 1g fiber, 26mg cholesterol, 130mg sodium

Chocolate Chip Cookies

Here's America's favorite cookie. You might want to bake a double batch, because they will disappear in no time.

active time 15 minutes   *bake time* 10 to 12 minutes per batch   *makes* 36 cookies

1¼ cups all-purpose flour
½ teaspoon baking soda
½ teaspoon salt
½ cup butter or margarine (1 stick), softened
½ cup packed light brown sugar
¾ cup granulated sugar
2 large eggs
1½ teaspoons vanilla extract
1 package (6 ounces) semisweet chocolate chips (1 cup)
2 cups pecans (8 ounces), chopped (optional)

1 Preheat oven to 375°F. In small bowl, combine flour, baking soda, and salt.

2 In large bowl, with mixer at medium speed, beat butter and brown and granulated sugars until light and fluffy. Beat in eggs and vanilla until well combined. Reduce speed to low; beat in flour mixture just until blended. With wooden spoon, stir in chocolate chips and pecans, if using.

3 Drop dough by rounded measuring tablespoons, 2 inches apart, on two ungreased cookie sheets. Bake until golden around edges, 10 to 12 minutes, rotating cookie sheets between upper and lower oven racks halfway through baking. With wide metal spatula, transfer cookies to wire racks to cool completely.

4 Repeat with remaining dough. Store cookies in cookie jar up to 1 week.

each cookie About 80 calories, 1g protein, 11g carbohydrate, 4g total fat (2g saturated), 1g fiber, 13 mg cholesterol, 79 mg sodium

cookie tip Be sure to keep similar cookies together—crisp cookies will get soggy if they're placed next to soft ones. Use separate cookie jars or Christmas tins, and avoid piling different cookies on top of one another on a platter.

Peanut Butter Cookies (recipe page 22), Chocolate Chip Cookies, and Chewy Molasses Spice Cookies (recipe page 24)

Peanut Butter Cookies

These cookies contain an entire jar of peanut butter—they couldn't get any more peanut buttery!

active time 40 minutes *bake time* 12 to 14 minutes per batch *makes* 72 cookies

2 cups all-purpose flour
1 teaspoon baking powder
1 teaspoon baking soda
1 teaspoon salt
1 cup butter (2 sticks), softened (no substitutions)
1 cup packed brown sugar
1 cup plus 2 tablespoons granulated sugar
1 teaspoon vanilla extract
2 large eggs
1 jar (18 ounces) creamy peanut butter

1 Preheat oven to 350°F. On waxed paper, combine flour, baking powder, baking soda, and salt.

2 In large bowl, with mixer on medium speed, beat butter, brown sugar, and 1 cup granulated sugar until creamy, 2 minutes, occasionally scraping bowl with rubber spatula. On low speed, beat in vanilla, then eggs, one at a time, beating well after each addition. Add peanut butter and beat on medium speed until creamy, 2 minutes. On low speed, beat in flour mixture just until blended, occasionally scraping bowl.

3 Drop dough by rounded measuring tablespoons, 2 inches apart, on ungreased large cookie sheet. Place remaining 2 tablespoons granulated sugar on plate or sheet of waxed paper. Dip tines of fork in sugar, then press twice into top of each cookie, making a criss-cross pattern (see opposite).

4 Bake until lightly browned at edges, 12 to 14 minutes. Cool cookies on cookie sheet 2 minutes. With wide metal spatula, transfer cookies to wire rack to cool completely. Repeat with remaining dough and granulated sugar.

5 Store cookies in cookie jar up to 1 week.

each cookie About 105 calories, 2g protein, 10g carbohydrate, 7g total fat (3g saturated), 1g fiber, 13mg cholesterol, 120mg sodium

Making Crosshatch Marks

Flattening peanut-butter cookie dough crisscross with a fork gives the cookies a pretty lattice pattern on top. Dip the tines of fork in red, green, or silver sugar first to add Christmas sparkle.

Chewy Molasses Spice Cookies

Dark and chewy, these luscious cookies originated in Europe centuries ago. Those early spice cookies were made with black pepper and mustard, just as ours are.

active time 15 minutes *bake time* 13 to 15 minutes per batch *makes* 42 cookies

- 2 cups all-purpose flour
- 1½ teaspoons baking soda
- 1 teaspoon ground ginger
- ¼ teaspoon ground cinnamon
- ¼ teaspoon salt
- ¼ teaspoon finely ground black pepper
- ⅛ teaspoon ground cloves
- ⅛ teaspoon dry mustard
- ½ cup butter or margarine (1 stick), softened
- ¾ cup packed dark brown sugar
- ½ cup light (mild) molasses
- 1 large egg
- 1 teaspoon vanilla extract

1 Preheat oven to 350°F. In small bowl, stir together flour, baking soda, ginger, cinnamon, salt, pepper, cloves, and mustard.

2 In large bowl, with mixer on medium speed, beat butter and brown sugar until smooth. Beat in molasses until combined. On low speed, beat in egg and vanilla until blended. Beat in flour mixture until combined, scraping bowl occasionally with rubber spatula.

3 Drop dough by rounded measuring tablespoons, 3 inches apart, on ungreased large cookie sheet. Bake until flattened and evenly browned, 13 to 15 minutes. Cool cookies on cookie sheet on wire rack 2 minutes. With wide metal spatula, transfer cookies to rack to cool completely. Repeat with remaining dough.

4 Store cookies in cookie jar up to 1 week.

each cookie About 70 calories, 1g protein, 11g carbohydrate, 2g total fat (1g saturated), 0g fiber, 11mg cholesterol, 85mg sodium

Ginger Cookies

Spicy, crunchy, gingery cookies, perfect for the holiday season, are particularly delicious paired with mugs of mulled cider.

active time 40 minutes   *bake time* 13 to 15 minutes per batch   *makes* 42 cookies

½ cup butter or margarine (1 stick)
¼ cup vegetable shortening
1 cup light (mild) molasses
1 tablespoon baking soda
3½ cups all-purpose flour
1 cup sugar
½ cup buttermilk
1 tablespoon ground ginger
¼ teaspoon salt

1 Preheat oven to 350°F. Grease two large cookie sheets.

2 In small saucepan, melt butter and shortening over medium-low heat, swirling pan occasionally.

3 In large bowl, with wire whisk, mix molasses and baking soda. Add butter mixture, flour, sugar, buttermilk, ginger, and salt and stir until blended.

4 Drop dough by rounded measuring table-spoons, 3 inches apart, on prepared cookie sheets. Bake 13 to 15 minutes, rotating cookie sheets between upper and lower racks halfway through baking. Cool cookies on cookie sheets 1 minute. With wide metal spatula, transfer cookies to wire racks to cool completely. Repeat with remaining dough.

5 Store cookies in cookie jar up to 1 week.

each cookie About 110 calories, 1g protein, 18g carbohydrate, 4g total fat (2g saturated), 0g fiber, 6mg cholesterol, 135mg sodium

Brown Sugar Pecan Crisps

These crunchy cookies deliver a lot of nutty taste with each bite, which is sure to make them a favorite among your Christmas crowd.

active time 1 hour 10 minutes   *bake time* 12 minutes per batch   *makes* 96 cookies

2½ cups all-purpose flour
½ teaspoon baking soda
½ teaspoon salt
2½ cups packed brown sugar
1 cup butter (2 sticks), softened
2 large eggs
1 teaspoon vanilla extract
1½ cups chopped pecans, plus halves for decorating (optional)
red sugar sprinkles for decorating (optional)

1 Preheat oven to 350°F. Line 4 cookie sheets with parchment paper.

2 In medium bowl, with wire whisk, stir flour, baking soda, and salt.

3 In large bowl, with mixer at medium speed, beat brown sugar and butter until creamy, occasionally scraping bowl. Beat in eggs, one at a time, beating well after each addition. Beat in vanilla. Reduce speed to low; gradually beat in flour mixture just until blended, occasionally scraping bowl. With wooden spoon, stir in chopped pecans.

4 Drop dough by rounded measuring teaspoons, 2 inches apart, onto prepared cookie sheets.

5 Bake cookies 12 minutes or until golden brown. If decorating, bake 6 minutes and remove from oven. Press pecan half in center of each cookie or sprinkle top with red sugar sprinkles. Bake 6 minutes longer or until golden brown. Transfer to wire racks to cool. Repeat with remaining dough. Store cookies in airtight containers at room temperature up to 1 week or in freezer up to 1 month.

each cookie About 60 calories, 1g protein, 8g carbohydrate, 3g total fat (1g saturated), 0g fiber, 9mg cholesterol, 20mg sodium

Sour-Cream Cookies

Subtle nutmeg flavor and a light, cakelike texture make these an elegant partner for a cup of afternoon tea.

active time 25 minutes   *bake time* 10 to 12 minutes per batch   *makes* 30 cookies

1¾ cups all-purpose flour
1 teaspoon baking powder
½ teaspoon salt
¼ teaspoon baking soda
¼ teaspoon ground nutmeg
½ cup butter or margarine (1 stick), softened
1 cup plus 2 tablespoons sugar
1 large egg
2 teaspoons vanilla extract
½ cup sour cream

1 Preheat oven to 400°F. Grease large cookie sheet.

2 In medium bowl, combine flour, baking powder, salt, baking soda, and nutmeg.

3 In large bowl, with mixer on medium speed, beat butter and 1 cup sugar until creamy, occasionally scraping bowl with rubber spatula. Beat in egg and vanilla, then sour cream, until well combined. On low speed, beat in flour mixture just until blended, occasionally scraping bowl.

4 Drop dough by rounded measuring tablespoons, 2 inches apart, on prepared cookie sheet. Sprinkle lightly with some of remaining sugar. Bake until edges are lightly browned, 10 to 12 minutes. With wide metal spatula, transfer cookies to wire rack to cool. Repeat with remaining dough and sugar.

5 Store cookies in cookie jar up to 1 week.

each cookie About 70 calories, 1g protein, 11g carbohydrate, 2g total fat (1g saturated), 0g fiber, 11mg cholesterol, 85mg sodium

Classic Oatmeal-Raisin Cookies

Ever since settlers brought oats west with them in the late 1700s, the oatmeal cookie (in many forms) has been an American favorite. This version is crisp on the outside and just a bit chewy in the center.

active time 25 minutes *bake time* 11 to 13 minutes per batch *makes* 72 cookies

1 cup all-purpose flour
2 teaspoons baking soda
½ teaspoon salt
1 cup packed brown sugar
½ cup butter or margarine (1 stick), softened
1 teaspoon vanilla extract
2 large eggs
3 cups old-fashioned or quick-cooking oats, uncooked
1½ cups dark seedless raisins

1 Preheat oven to 350°F. Line large cookie sheet with nonstick foil (or use nonstick cookie sheet).

2 On waxed paper, combine flour, baking soda, and salt.

3 In large bowl, with mixer on medium speed, beat brown sugar and butter until creamy, occasionally scraping bowl with rubber spatula. Beat in vanilla, then eggs, one at a time, beating well after each addition. On low speed, gradually add flour mixture; beat just until blended, occasionally scraping bowl. With spoon, stir in oats and raisins.

4 Drop dough by heaping measuring teaspoons, 2 inches apart, onto prepared cookie sheet. Bake until tops are golden, 11 to 13 minutes. Cool cookies on cookie sheet 1 minute. With wide metal spatula, transfer cookies to wire rack to cool completely. Repeat with remaining dough.

5 Store cookies in cookie jar up to 1 week.

each cookie About 70 calories, 2g protein, 12g carbohydrate, 2g total fat (1g saturated), 1g fiber, 10mg cholesterol, 70mg sodium

Coconut-Oatmeal Crisps

Chewy oatmeal cookies get sweet and crispy with the addition of rice cereal and coconut.

active time 30 minutes *bake time* 11 to 13 minutes per batch *makes* 66 cookies

1 cup all-purpose flour
1 teaspoon baking powder
1 teaspoon baking soda
1 cup butter or margarine (2 sticks), softened
¾ cup granulated sugar
¾ cup packed brown sugar
2 teaspoons vanilla extract
2 large eggs
2 cups old-fashioned oats, uncooked
2 cups crispy rice cereal
1 cup sweetened flaked coconut

1 Preheat oven to 350°F. Grease large cookie sheet. On waxed paper, combine flour, baking powder, and baking soda.

2 In large bowl, with mixer on medium speed, beat butter and sugars until creamy, about 2 minutes, occasionally scraping bowl with rubber spatula. On low speed, beat in vanilla, then eggs, one at a time, beating well after each addition. Gradually add flour mixture; beat just until blended, occasionally scraping bowl with rubber spatula. With spoon, stir in oats, cereal, and coconut.

3 Drop dough by rounded measuring tablespoons, 3 inches apart, onto prepared cookie sheet. Bake until tops are golden, 11 to 13 minutes. With wide metal spatula, transfer cookies to wire rack to cool completely. Repeat with remaining dough.

4 Store cookies in cookie jar up to 2 weeks.

each cookie About 70 calories, 1g protein, 9g carbohydrate, 4g total fat (2g saturated), 0g fiber, 14mg cholesterol, 65mg sodium

Healthy Makeover Chocolate-Chip Oatmeal Cookies

Revamped, these gems are still ooey-gooey good—but they're only 80 calories each (with a gram of healthy fiber per cookie). We've also cut out half the fat and cholesterol you'd find in this treat's calorie-laden cousins. Your guests will be thrilled to indulge!

active time 15 minutes *bake time* 12 to 13 minutes per batch *makes* 48 cookies

½ cup packed brown sugar
½ cup granulated sugar
½ cup trans-fat-free vegetable oil spread (60% to 70% oil)
1 large egg
1 large egg white
2 teaspoons vanilla extract
1¼ cups all-purpose flour
1 teaspoon baking soda
½ teaspoon salt
2½ cups old-fashioned or quick-cooking oats, uncooked
1 package (6 ounces) bittersweet (62% cacao) or semisweet chocolate chips (1 cup)

1 Preheat oven to 350°F.

2 In large bowl, with mixer on medium-low speed, beat sugars and vegetable spread until well blended, occasionally scraping bowl with rubber spatula. Add egg, egg white, and vanilla; beat until smooth. Beat in flour, baking soda, and salt until mixed. With spoon, stir in oats and chocolate chips until well combined.

3 Drop dough by rounded measuring tablespoons, 2 inches apart, on ungreased large cookie sheet. Bake until golden, 12 to 13 minutes. With wide metal spatula, transfer cookies to wire rack to cool completely. Repeat with remaining dough.

4 Store cookies in cookie jar up to 3 days.

each cookie About 80 calories, 1g protein, 11g carbohydrate, 4g total fat (1g saturated), 1g fiber, 4mg cholesterol, 70mg sodium

Apricot Oatmeal Cookies

These cookies are chock-full of sweet, tart, chewy, crunchy ingredients!

active time 40 minutes   *bake time* 14 to 15 minutes per batch   *makes* 54 cookies

1 cup butter or margarine (2 sticks), softened
1 cup packed light brown sugar
½ cup granulated sugar
2 large eggs
1½ cups all-purpose flour
1 teaspoon baking soda
1 teaspoon ground cinnamon
1 teaspoon almond extract
½ teaspoon salt
3 cups old-fashioned or quick-cooking oats, uncooked
1 cup chopped dried apricots
¾ cup dried cranberries
¾ cup sweetened flaked coconut
¾ cup slivered almonds, toasted (see opposite)

1 Preheat oven to 350°F.

2 In large bowl, with mixer on medium speed, beat butter and sugars until creamy, 2 minutes, occasionally scraping bowl with rubber spatula. On low speed, beat in eggs, flour, baking soda, cinnamon, almond extract, and salt just until blended. Stir in oats, dried fruit, coconut, and almonds.

3 Drop dough by rounded measuring tablespoons, 2 inches apart, onto ungreased large cookie sheet. Bake until tops are golden, 14 to 15 minutes. Using a wide metal spatula, transfer cookies to wire racks to cool. Repeat with remaining dough.

4 Store cookies in cookie jar up to 1 week.

each cookie About 130 calories, 3g protein, 18g carbohydrate, 6g total fat (3g saturated), 2g fiber, 18mg cholesterol, 85mg sodium

Toasting Nuts

Toasting nuts brings out their flavor, and in the case of nuts such as hazelnuts, allows the skins to be removed.

To toast almonds, pecans, walnuts, cashews, or hazelnuts,
preheat oven to 350°F. Spread shelled nuts in a single layer on a cookie sheet. Bake, stirring occasionally, until lightly browned and fragrant, 10 minutes. Toast hazelnuts until skins begin to peel away. Let nuts cool completely before chopping.

To skin hazelnuts,
wrap the still-warm toasted nuts in a clean kitchen towel and let stand for 10 minutes. Using towel, rub to remove as much skin as possible (all of the skin may not come off).

cookie tip

Avoid traveling with fragile buttery cookies that can disintegrate en route. Opt for heftier varieties, such as Cranberry-Chocolate Chunk Cookies (page 40) or Figgy Bars (page 114).

Oatmeal-Chocolate-Cherry Cookies

For chewy cookies, bake the minimum time—for a crispy treat, bake a few minutes longer.

active time 35 minutes   *bake time* 12 to 14 minutes per batch   *makes* 54 cookies

1½ cups all-purpose flour
2 teaspoons baking soda
½ teaspoon salt
¾ cup granulated sugar
¾ cup packed brown sugar
¾ cup butter or margarine (1½ sticks), softened
2 teaspoons vanilla extract
2 large eggs
3 cups old-fashioned oats, uncooked
1 cup dried tart cherries or raisins
1 package (6 ounces) semisweet chocolate chips (1 cup)

1 Preheat oven to 350°F. Grease large cookie sheet.

2 On waxed paper, combine flour, baking soda, and salt.

3 In large bowl, with mixer on medium speed, beat sugars and butter until creamy, occasionally scraping bowl with rubber spatula. Beat in vanilla, then eggs, one at a time, beating well after each addition. On low speed, gradually beat in flour mixture just until blended, occasionally scraping bowl with spatula. With spoon, stir in oats, dried fruit, and chocolate chips.

4 Drop dough by rounded measuring tablespoons, 2 inches apart, onto prepared cookie sheet. Bake until tops are golden, 12 to 14 minutes. With wide metal spatula, transfer cookies to wire racks to cool completely. Repeat with remaining dough.

5 Store cookies in cookie jar up to 1 week.

each cookie About 100 calories, 1g protein, 15g carbohydrate, 4g total fat (2g saturated), 1g fiber, 15mg cholesterol, 100mg sodium

Thumbprint Jammies

Make a rainbow batch of these old-fashioned favorites, using several different kinds of jam. You can even try mint jelly for a fun surprise.

active time 20 minutes *bake time* 18 to 20 minutes per batch *makes* 30 cookies

- 2 **cups all-purpose flour**
- 1 **teaspoon baking powder**
- ¼ **teaspoon salt**
- 1 **cup sugar**
- ¾ **cup butter or margarine (1½ sticks), softened**
- 1 **large egg**
- 3 **tablespoons milk**
- 2 **teaspoons vanilla extract**
- ⅓ **cup favorite seedless jam**

1 Preheat oven to 350°F. On waxed paper, combine flour, baking powder, and salt.

2 In large bowl, with mixer on medium speed, beat sugar and butter until creamy. Add egg, milk, and vanilla; beat until well blended. On low speed, beat in flour mixture just until blended.

3 Drop dough by rounded measuring tablespoons, 2 inches apart, onto ungreased large cookie sheet. Bake 6 minutes. Remove cookie sheet from oven. Working quickly, with greased rounded measuring teaspoon or large end of melon baller, gently make a small indentation in center of each cookie, making sure not to press all the way through. Fill each indentation with rounded ½ teaspoon jam.

4 Return cookies to oven and bake until edges are browned, 12 to 14 minutes longer. With wide metal spatula, transfer cookies to wire rack to cool. Repeat with remaining dough and jam.

5 Store cookies in cookie jar up to 1 week.

each cookie About 120 calories, 1g protein, 18g carbohydrate, 5g total fat (3g saturated), 0g fiber, 20mg cholesterol, 90mg sodium

cookie tip

The easiest way to get lots of jam into the center of these kid-friendly favorites is to use the back of a melon baller or measuring spoon to make the "thumbprint."

Applesauce-Raisin Cookies with Lemon Glaze

A Granny Smith apple adds moisture and texture, while lemon glaze gives an appealing shine to these old-fashioned beauties.

active time 35 minutes *bake time* 20 to 22 minutes per batch *makes* 42 cookies

Cookies

- 2 cups all-purpose flour
- ½ teaspoon baking powder
- ½ teaspoon baking soda
- ½ teaspoon ground cinnamon
- ¼ teaspoon ground allspice
- ¼ teaspoon salt
- ½ cup butter or margarine (1 stick), softened
- ½ cup granulated sugar
- ¼ cup packed brown sugar
- 1 large egg
- 1 cup unsweetened applesauce
- 1 teaspoon vanilla extract
- 1 medium Granny Smith apple, cored and finely chopped
- 1 cup dark seedless raisins
- 1 cup walnuts (4 ounces), coarsely chopped (optional)

1 Preheat oven to 375°F. Grease two large cookie sheets.

2 Prepare cookies: On waxed paper, combine flour, baking powder, baking soda, cinnamon, allspice, and salt.

3 In large bowl, with mixer on medium speed, beat butter and sugars until light and fluffy. On low speed, beat in egg, applesauce, and vanilla until well combined. Beat in flour mixture just until blended. With spoon, stir in apple, raisins, and walnuts, if using.

4 Drop dough by rounded measuring tablespoons, 1 inch apart, on prepared cookie sheets. Bake until lightly browned around edges and set, 20 to 22 minutes, rotating cookie sheets between upper and lower oven racks halfway through baking.

5 While cookies bake, prepare glaze: In small bowl, stir confectioners' sugar and lemon juice until smooth.

6 With wide metal spatula, transfer cookies to wire racks. With pastry brush, spread glaze over warm cookies; cool completely.

7 Store cookies in cookie jar up to 3 days.

each cookie About 80 calories, 1g protein, 14g carbohydrate, 2g total fat (1g saturated), 0g fiber, 11mg cholesterol, 55mg sodium

Lemon Glaze

1 **cup confectioners' sugar**
2 **tablespoons fresh lemon juice (see below)**

cookie tip | To get the most juice, zap your lemon in the microwave on High for about 20 seconds or until it's barely warm to the touch. Just before cutting, roll it on the countertop. The combination of warming and rolling will release more juice from the lemon.

Cranberry-Chocolate Chunk Cookies

This is a chewy, chunky take on a classic chocolate chip cookie, with the welcome holiday flavor of cranberries.

active time 30 minutes *bake time* 11 to 13 minutes plus cooling *makes* 36 cookies

2½ cups all-purpose flour
1 teaspoon baking soda
½ teaspoon salt
¾ cup butter or margarine (1½ sticks), softened
¾ cup packed dark brown sugar
¼ cup granulated sugar
3 tablespoons light corn syrup
2 large eggs
2 teaspoons vanilla extract
1¼ cups walnuts, toasted (see page 33) and chopped
1 cup dried cranberries
4 ounces white chocolate, chopped
4 ounces semisweet chocolate, chopped

1 Arrange 2 oven racks in upper and lower thirds of oven. Preheat oven to 375°F. Line 3 cookie sheets with parchment paper.

2 On waxed paper, combine flour, baking soda, and salt; set aside. In large bowl, with mixer on medium speed, beat butter, sugars, and corn syrup until just creamy. Beat in eggs and vanilla until blended. Reduce speed to low. In 2 batches, add flour mixture, beating between batches until just blended. Stir in two-thirds of walnuts, cranberries, and chocolate pieces. Refrigerate dough 15 minutes or up to 1 day.

3 Drop dough by rounded tablespoons, 2 inches apart, on prepared cookie sheets (return remaining dough to refrigerator for next batch). Bake 5 minutes. Working quickly, press some of remaining nuts, cranberries, and chocolate pieces into cookies. Rotate sheets on racks; bake 6 to 8 minutes longer or until edges are golden brown.

4 Transfer cookies to wire rack to cool completely. Repeat with remaining dough. Store cookies, layered with waxed paper, in airtight containers for up to 1 week or in freezer for up to 1 month.

each cookie About 170 calories, 2g protein, 21g carbohydrate, 9g total fat (4g saturated), 1g fiber, 21mg cholesterol, 75mg sodium

White Chocolate–Peppermint Chippers

These colorful cookies are a perfect choice for the holiday cookie jar.

active time 30 minutes   *bake time* 10 to 12 minutes per batch   *makes* 66 cookies

¾ cup white chocolate chips

2 cups all-purpose flour

½ teaspoon baking powder

½ teaspoon salt

¾ cup butter or margarine (1½ sticks), softened

⅔ cup sugar

1 large egg

1 teaspoon vanilla extract

12 round hard peppermint candies

¾ cup sweet dark chocolate chips, such as Hershey's Special Dark Chocolate Chips

1 In large microwave-safe bowl, melt ⅓ cup white chocolate chips as label directs. Cool slightly.

2 Meanwhile, preheat oven to 375°F. Grease large cookie sheet. On waxed paper, combine flour, baking powder, and salt.

3 Add butter to melted chocolate; with mixer on medium speed, beat until creamy. Add sugar and beat until fluffy, occasionally scraping bowl with rubber spatula. Add egg and vanilla and beat until well blended. On low speed, beat in flour mixture just until blended.

4 Place candies in zip-tight plastic bag and coarsely crush with rolling pin. With spoon, stir candies, dark chocolate chips, and remaining white chocolate chips into dough until combined.

5 Drop dough by rounded measuring teaspoons, 2 inches apart, onto prepared cookie sheet. Bake until golden brown at edges, 10 to 12 minutes. Cool cookies on cookie sheet on wire rack 1 minute. With wide metal spatula, transfer cookies to rack to cool completely. Repeat with remaining dough.

6 Store cookies in cookie jar up to 1 week.

each cookie About 70 calories, 1g protein, 8g carbohydrate, 4g total fat (2g saturated), 0g fiber, 10mg cholesterol, 45mg sodium

Apricot Fudgies

White chocolate chunks and pieces of dried apricot are a delightful surprise in these rich, fudgy cookies.

active time 30 minutes *bake time* 13 to 15 minutes per batch *makes* 36 cookies

8 squares (8 ounces) semisweet chocolate, coarsely chopped

6 tablespoons butter or margarine, cut into small pieces

¾ cup sugar

2 teaspoons vanilla extract

2 large eggs

¼ cup all-purpose flour

¼ cup unsweetened cocoa

½ teaspoon baking powder

¼ teaspoon salt

6 ounces white chocolate, Swiss confectionery bar, or white baking bar, coarsely chopped

1 cup dried apricot halves (8 ounces), coarsely chopped

1 Preheat oven to 350°F.

2 In 3-quart saucepan, melt semisweet chocolate and butter over low heat, stirring frequently. Remove saucepan from heat and, with wire whisk, stir in sugar and vanilla until blended. Whisk in eggs, one at a time, until mixture is smooth. With spoon, stir in flour, cocoa, baking powder, and salt until combined. Add white chocolate pieces and apricots; stir just until evenly mixed (dough will be loose and sticky—similar to brownie batter).

3 Drop dough by rounded measuring tablespoons, 1½ inches apart, onto ungreased large cookie sheet. Bake until tops of cookies are set, 13 to 15 minutes. Cool cookies on cookie sheet on wire rack 30 seconds. With wide metal spatula, transfer cookies to rack to cool completely. Repeat with remaining dough.

4 Store cookies in cookie jar up to 3 days.

each cookie About 110 calories, 2g protein, 14g carbohydrate, 6g total fat (3g saturated), 1g fiber, 13mg cholesterol, 55mg sodium

Chocolate Wows

The name says it all! Three kinds of chocolate plus pecans make a spectacular cookie.

active time 20 minutes *bake time* 13 minutes per batch *makes* 48 cookies

⅓ cup all-purpose flour
¼ cup unsweetened cocoa
1 teaspoon baking powder
¼ teaspoon salt
6 squares (6 ounces) semisweet chocolate, chopped
½ cup butter or margarine (1 stick)
2 large eggs
¾ cup sugar
1½ teaspoons vanilla extract
2 cups pecans (8 ounces), chopped
1 package (6 ounces) semisweet chocolate chips (1 cup)

1 Preheat oven to 325°F. Grease two large cookie sheets. In small bowl, combine flour, cocoa, baking powder, and salt.

2 In heavy 2-quart saucepan over low heat, melt chocolate and butter, stirring frequently, until smooth. Let cool.

3 In large bowl, with mixer on medium speed, beat eggs and sugar until light and lemon colored, 2 minutes, frequently scraping bowl with rubber spatula. Add cooled chocolate mixture, flour mixture, and vanilla; on low speed, beat just until blended. Increase speed to medium; beat 2 minutes. With wooden spoon, stir in pecans and chocolate chips.

4 Drop dough by rounded measuring teaspoons, 2 inches apart, on prepared cookie sheets. With small metal spatula or back of spoon, spread dough into 2-inch rounds (see opposite). Bake until tops are shiny and cracked, 13 minutes, rotating cookie sheets between upper and lower oven racks halfway through baking. Cool cookies on cookie sheet 10 minutes. With wide metal spatula, transfer cookies to wire racks to cool completely. Repeat with remaining dough.

5 Store cookies in cookie jar up to 3 days.

each cookie About 100 calories, 1g protein, 9g carbohydrate, 7g total fat (3g saturated), 1g fiber, 14mg cholesterol, 45mg sodium

Flattening Stiff Cookie Dough

A stiff cookie dough will bake more evenly if flattened slightly with a small metal spatula after it is dropped onto the cookie sheet.

Triple-Chocolate Chubbies

We added more chocolate, walnuts, and pecans to a dense brownie-like batter to create a big, fat cookie that became an instant hit in our test kitchen. You'll need a really big Christmas cookie tin to accommodate these bad boys.

active time 25 minutes *bake time* 14 minutes per batch *makes* 24 cookies

¼ cup all-purpose flour
¼ cup unsweetened cocoa
½ teaspoon baking powder
¼ teaspoon salt
8 squares (8 ounces) semisweet chocolate, chopped
6 tablespoons butter or margarine, cut into pieces
1 cup sugar
2 teaspoons vanilla extract
2 large eggs
1 package (6 ounces) semisweet chocolate chips (1 cup)
½ cup pecans, chopped
½ cup walnuts, chopped

1 Preheat oven to 350°F. In small bowl, stir together flour, cocoa, baking powder, and salt.

2 In 3-quart saucepan, melt chopped chocolate and butter over low heat, stirring frequently, until smooth. Pour into large bowl; cool to lukewarm. Stir in sugar and vanilla until blended. Stir in eggs, one at a time, until well blended. Add flour mixture and stir until combined (batter will be thin). Stir in chocolate chips, pecans, and walnuts.

3 Drop dough by heaping measuring tablespoons, 1½ inches apart, on ungreased large cookie sheet. Bake until set, 14 minutes. Cool cookies on cookie sheet on wire rack 2 minutes. With wide metal spatula, carefully transfer cookies to rack to cool completely.

4 Store cookies in cookie jar up to 3 days.

each cookie About 180 calories, 2g protein, 21g carbohydrate, 11g total fat (5g saturated), 1g fiber, 26mg cholesterol, 70mg sodium

Coconut Macaroons

These flourless cookies are a welcome holiday treat for people who are allergic to wheat or gluten.

active time 10 minutes *bake time* 25 minutes per batch *makes* 42 cookies

3 cups sweetened flaked coconut
¾ cup sugar
4 large egg whites
¼ teaspoon salt
1 teaspoon vanilla extract
⅛ teaspoon almond extract

1 Preheat oven to 325°F. Line two large cookie sheets with parchment paper or foil.

2 In large bowl, stir coconut, sugar, egg whites, salt, and vanilla and almond extracts until well combined.

3 Drop dough by rounded measuring teaspoons, 1 inch apart, on prepared cookie sheets. Bake until set and lightly golden, 25 minutes, rotating cookie sheets between upper and lower oven racks halfway through baking. Cool cookies on cookie sheets 1 minute. With wide metal spatula, transfer cookies to racks to cool completely.

4 Store cookies in cookie jar up to 3 days.

each cookie About 40 calories, 1g protein, 6g carbohydrate, 2g total fat (2g saturated), 0.5g fiber, 0mg cholesterol, 32mg sodium

chocolate-coconut macaroons

Prepare as directed, stirring **2 tablespoons unsweetened cocoa** and **1 square (1 ounce) semisweet chocolate, grated,** into coconut mixture in step 2.

Chocolate-Hazelnut Macaroons

Chocolate and hazelnut is a delectable flavor combination. Although these chewy-crisp (and gluten-free) cookies are delicious on their own, you can make them even more elegant by sandwiching two together with some melted chocolate.

active time 30 minutes *bake time* 10 minutes per batch *makes* 30 cookies

1 cup hazelnuts (filberts; 5 ounces)
1 cup sugar
¼ cup unsweetened cocoa
1 square (1 ounce) unsweetened chocolate, chopped
⅛ teaspoon salt
2 large egg whites
1 teaspoon vanilla extract

1 Preheat oven to 350°F. Toast and skin hazelnuts (page 33). Line two large cookie sheets with foil.

2 In food processor with knife blade attached, process hazelnuts, sugar, cocoa, chocolate, and salt until nuts and chocolate are finely ground. Add egg whites and vanilla and process until blended.

3 Drop dough by rounded measuring tea-spoons, using another spoon to release dough, 2 inches apart, on prepared cookie sheets. Bake until tops feel firm when pressed lightly, 10 minutes, rotating cookie sheets between upper and lower oven racks halfway through baking. Cool cookies on cookie sheets on wire racks. Repeat with remaining dough.

4 Store cookies in cookie jar up to 3 days.

each cookie About 60 calories, 1g protein, 8g carbohydrate, 3g total fat (1g saturated), 0.5g fiber, 0mg cholesterol, 15mg sodium

Shaped Cookies

Preparing shaped cookies is a great way to get kids in on the act. They'll love rolling the dough into small balls and dipping them in sugar, as well as helping to shape the biscotti. Biscotti dough is first formed into a log and baked, then sliced and baked again, yielding terrifically crispy, crunchy cookies that are just right for dunking in coffee. Some doughs for shaped cookies need a short turn in the fridge to firm up just a bit; check the individual recipes.

Whole-Grain Gingersnaps (recipe page 61), Best Linzer Cookies (recipe page 70), and Mint Brownie Bites (recipe page 53)

Here are a few tips for shaped cookie success:

Even if you've chilled the dough, work quickly when rolling it into balls. You want the butterfat in the dough to stay as cold as possible before it hits the heat of the oven, so the cookies will hold their shape better. To keep the dough cool, you might want to stick it in the refrigerator between batches.

For even baking, try to scoop the same amount of dough for each cookie. "Shape dough by rounded teaspoons" or "Shape dough by rounded tablespoons" means you should use a measuring teaspoon or tablespoon, not a spoon for stirring tea or a cereal or soupspoon.

If the dough starts to stick to your hands, try rubbing them with a little flour or vegetable oil.

If the dough gets crumbly, moisten your hands with water, then gather the dough together, pressing it into a disk.

Mint Brownie Bites

These rich little brownies, topped with a cool peppermint, are an unexpected treat at holiday time.

active time 35 minutes plus cooling *bake time* 7 to 8 minutes per batch *makes* 24 cookies

Brownie Bites
- ⅔ **cup all-purpose flour**
- ½ **cup unsweetened cocoa**
- ½ **teaspoon baking powder**
- **pinch salt**
- ¾ **cup granulated sugar**
- 3 **tablespoons butter or margarine, melted and cooled**
- 2 **tablespoons honey**
- 1 **teaspoon vanilla extract**
- 1 **large egg white**

Topping
- 1 **cup confectioners' sugar**
- 1 **tablespoon milk**
- 1 **tablespoon butter or margarine, softened**
- ½ **teaspoon peppermint extract**
- 2 **ounces white chocolate, melted and cooled**
- 2 **ounces round hard peppermint candies, broken into chunks**

1 Prepare Brownie Bites: Preheat oven to 350°F. Grease large cookie sheet.

2 In large bowl, combine flour, cocoa, baking powder, and salt. In medium bowl, whisk sugar, butter, honey, vanilla, and egg white until blended. Stir sugar mixture into flour mixture; then, with hand, press dough until just blended.

3 With greased hands, shape dough into 1-inch balls and place on prepared cookie sheet 2 inches apart; press to flatten slightly. Bake 7 to 8 minutes or until brownies have cracked slightly. Transfer to wire rack to cool.

4 Prepare Topping: In medium bowl, whisk confectioners' sugar and milk until smooth. Whisk in butter and extract, then whisk in melted chocolate until smooth. Swirl 1 teaspoon topping on each cookie. Top each frosted cookie with 1 candy piece. Store in tightly sealed container with waxed paper between layers at room temperature up to 3 days or in freezer up to 1 month.

each cookie **About 105 calories, 1g protein, 20g carbohydrate, 3g total fat (2g saturated), 1g fiber, 6mg cholesterol, 40mg sodium**

Chocolate Crinkles

This cookie takes its name from its interesting shape. As the rich, sugar-coated dough bakes, it spreads into puffy rounds with small cracks on top and is topped with a snowlike coating of sugar.

active time 25 minutes plus chilling *bake time* 8 minutes per batch *makes* 48 cookies

¾ cup plus 2 tablespoons all-purpose flour
¼ cup unsweetened cocoa
½ teaspoon baking soda
¼ teaspoon baking powder
⅛ teaspoon salt
4 tablespoons butter or margarine, softened
½ cup plus 2 tablespoons granulated sugar
1 tablespoon light corn syrup
1 square (1 ounce) unsweetened chocolate, melted and cooled
1 large egg
1 teaspoon vanilla extract
¼ cup confectioners' sugar

1 In small bowl, stir together flour, cocoa, baking soda, baking powder, and salt.

2 In large bowl, with mixer on medium speed, beat butter, granulated sugar, and corn syrup until combined. On low speed, beat in chocolate, egg, and vanilla until well blended. Beat in flour mixture until combined, scraping bowl occasionally with rubber spatula. Cover bowl with plastic wrap and refrigerate 1 hour.

3 Preheat oven to 350°F. Place confectioners' sugar in small bowl. With hands, shape dough into 1-inch balls; roll in confectioners' sugar. Place balls, 1 inch apart, on ungreased large cookie sheet. Bake until set, 8 minutes. With wide metal spatula, transfer cookies to wire rack to cool completely. Repeat with remaining dough and confectioners' sugar.

4 Store cookies in cookie jar up to 1 week.

each cookie About 35 calories, 1g protein, 6g carbohydrate, 1g total fat (1g saturated), 0.5g fiber, 7mg cholesterol, 35mg sodium

Chocolate Sambuca Cookies

This seriously chocolate cookie, spiked with sambuca liqueur, makes an elegant after-dinner confection for an adults-only Christmas dinner.

active time 30 minutes plus chilling *bake time* 10 to 12 minutes per batch
makes 48 cookies

12 squares (12 ounces) semisweet chocolate, chopped
 4 tablespoons butter or margarine
 3 large eggs
⅓ cup sambuca (anise-flavored liqueur)
 1 cup granulated sugar
 1 cup blanched almonds (4 ounces), finely ground
⅔ cup all-purpose flour
¾ teaspoon baking soda
⅓ cup confectioners' sugar

1 In 2-quart saucepan, melt chocolate and butter over low heat, stirring frequently, until smooth. Let cool slightly.

2 In medium bowl, with wire whisk, mix eggs, sambuca, and ½ cup granulated sugar; blend in chocolate mixture. With spoon, stir ground almonds, flour, and baking soda into chocolate mixture until combined (dough will be very soft). Cover bowl with plastic wrap and refrigerate 4 hours or overnight.

3 Preheat oven to 350°F. In small bowl, combine confectioners' sugar and remaining ½ cup granulated sugar. With lightly floured hands, roll dough by rounded measuring table-spoons into 1-inch balls. Roll balls in sugar to coat and place about 2 inches apart, on ungreased large cookie sheet. Bake until cookies are just set and look puffed and cracked, 10 to 12 minutes. Cool on cookie sheet on wire rack 1 minute. With wide metal spatula, transfer to rack to cool completely. Repeat with remaining dough and sugar.

4 Store cookies in cookie jar up to 3 days.

each cookie About 85 calories, 2g protein, 12g carbohydrate, 4g total fat (0g saturated), 1g fiber, 13mg cholesterol, 20mg sodium

Melt-Aways

The name tells it all—these cookies melt in your mouth.

active time 25 minutes plus chilling *bake time* 19 to 22 minutes per batch
makes 42 cookies

2 cups all-purpose flour
¼ cup cornstarch
⅛ teaspoon salt
1 cup butter (2 sticks), softened (no substitutions)
2 cups confectioners' sugar
2 teaspoons vanilla extract

1 Preheat oven to 325°F. On waxed paper, combine flour, cornstarch, and salt.

2 In large bowl, with mixer on medium speed, beat butter until creamy. Beat in 1 cup confectioners' sugar until light and fluffy. On low speed, beat in flour mixture, then vanilla. Cover bowl with plastic and refrigerate 1 hour.

3 With hands, shape dough by heaping measuring teaspoons into 1-inch balls. Place balls, 1 inch apart, on ungreased large cookie sheet. Bake until set and lightly golden around edges, 19 to 22 minutes. With wide metal spatula, transfer to wire rack to cool slightly.

4 Sift remaining 1 cup confectioners' sugar into medium bowl. While cookies are still warm, roll in sugar to coat; return to rack to cool completely. When cool, gently roll cookies in sugar again. Repeat with remaining dough and sugar.

5 Store cookies in cookie jar up to 1 week.

each cookie About 90 calories, 1g protein, 11g carbohydrate, 5g total fat (3g saturated), 0g fiber, 13mg cholesterol, 55mg sodium

Snickerdoodles

For extra flavor, we added aromatic spices to these crackle-topped New England treats.

active time 30 minutes *bake time* 12 to 14 minutes per batch *makes* 42 cookies

3¼ cups all-purpose flour

2 teaspoons cream of tartar

1 teaspoon baking soda

1 teaspoon ground ginger

1 teaspoon ground cinnamon

½ teaspoon salt

1⅓ cups granulated sugar

1 cup butter or margarine (2 sticks), softened

¼ cup light (mild) molasses

1 teaspoon vanilla extract

1 large egg

½ cup coarse sugar

1 Preheat oven to 375°F. In medium bowl, mix flour, cream of tartar, baking soda, ginger, cinnamon, and salt until blended.

2 In large bowl, with mixer on medium speed, beat granulated sugar and butter until creamy, occasionally scraping bowl with rubber spatula. Beat in molasses, vanilla, and egg. On low speed, gradually add flour mixture just until blended, occasionally scraping bowl.

3 With hands, shape dough by rounded measuring tablespoons into 1½-inch balls. Roll balls in coarse sugar to coat. Place balls, 2 inches apart, on ungreased large cookie sheet. Bake until lightly golden and crinkly on top, 12 to 14 minutes. Cool cookies on cookie sheet on wire rack 1 minute. With wide metal spatula, transfer to rack to cool completely. Repeat with remaining dough and coarse sugar.

4 Store cookies in cookie jar up to 1 week.

each cookie About 115 calories, 1g protein, 17g carbohydrate, 5g total fat (3g saturated), 0g fiber, 18mg cholesterol, 105mg sodium

cookie tip When you present a tin of favorite cookies as a gift, affix a recipe card to the inside of the lid so the recipient can whip up her own batch.

Chipperdoodles

This variation on the Snickerdoodle (page 59) has mini chocolate chips added to the dough.

active time 25 minutes *bake time* 13 to 15 minutes per batch *makes* 42 cookies

3 cups all-purpose flour
2 teaspoons cream of tartar
1 teaspoon baking soda
½ teaspoon salt
1 cup butter or margarine (2 sticks), softened
1¼ cups plus 3 tablespoons sugar
½ teaspoon vanilla extract
2 large eggs
1 cup mini chocolate chips
2 teaspoons ground cinnamon

1 Preheat oven to 375°F. On waxed paper, combine flour, cream of tartar, baking soda, and salt.

2 In large bowl, with mixer on medium speed, beat butter and 1¼ cups sugar until creamy, occasionally scraping bowl with rubber spatula. Beat in vanilla, then eggs, one at a time, beating well after each addition. On low speed, gradually add flour mixture; beat just until blended, occasionally scraping bowl. With spoon, stir in chocolate chips.

3 In small bowl, combine cinnamon and remaining 3 tablespoons sugar. With hands, shape dough by rounded measuring tablespoons into 1½-inch balls. Roll each ball in cinnamon sugar. Place balls, 2 inches apart, on ungreased large cookie sheet. Using flat-bottomed glass, press balls slightly to make 2-inch rounds. Bake until pale golden and firm, 13 to 15 minutes. With wide metal spatula, transfer cookies to wire rack to cool. Repeat with remaining dough and cinnamon sugar.

4 Store cookies in cookie jar up to 1 week.

each cookie About 125 calories, 2g protein, 16g carbohydrate, 6g total fat (4g saturated), 1g fiber, 23mg cholesterol, 110mg sodium

Whole-Grain Gingersnaps

These festive treats are not just pretty—you'll get a dose of whole-wheat goodness in these spicy gingersnaps.

active time 25 minutes plus chilling   *bake time* 9 to 11 minutes per batch
makes 42 cookies

1 cup all-purpose flour
1 cup whole-wheat flour
1 teaspoon ground ginger
1 teaspoon baking soda
½ teaspoon ground cinnamon
½ teaspoon salt
½ cup sugar
6 tablespoons trans-fat-free vegetable oil spread (60% to 70% oil)
1 large egg
½ cup dark molasses
nonpareils or round white sprinkles (optional)

1 On sheet of waxed paper, combine flours, ginger, baking soda, cinnamon, and salt.

2 In large bowl, with mixer on low speed, beat sugar and vegetable oil spread until blended. Increase speed to high; beat until light and creamy, occasionally scraping bowl with rubber spatula. Beat in egg and molasses. On low speed, beat in flour mixture just until blended. Cover bowl with plastic wrap and refrigerate until easier to handle (dough will be slightly sticky), 1 hour.

3 Preheat oven to 350°F. With lightly greased hands, shape cookie dough by heaping measuring teaspoons into 1-inch balls. If desired, dip top of each ball in nonpareils. Place balls, 2½ inches apart, on ungreased large cookie sheet. Bake until tops are slightly cracked, 9 to 11 minutes. (Cookies will be very soft.) Cool cookies on cookie sheet on wire rack 1 minute. With wide metal spatula, transfer cookies to rack to cool completely. Repeat with remaining dough and nonpareils if using.

4 Store cookies in cookie jar up to 3 days.

each cookie About 55 calories, 1g protein, 9g carbohydrate, 2g total fat (0g saturated), 1g fiber, 5mg cholesterol, 75mg sodium

Molasses Cookies

An old-time favorite. Everyone will enjoy rolling the spicy dough into balls and dipping them in sugar.

active time 40 minutes plus chilling   *bake time* 10 to 12 minutes per batch
makes 72 cookies

- ¾ cup butter or margarine (1½ sticks)
- ¼ cup light (mild) molasses
- 1¼ cups sugar
- 1 large egg
- 2 cups all-purpose flour
- 2 teaspoons baking soda
- 1 teaspoon ground cinnamon
- ½ teaspoon ground ginger
- ½ teaspoon salt
- ¼ teaspoon ground cloves

1 Preheat oven to 375°F.

2 In 3-quart saucepan, melt butter over low heat. Remove saucepan from heat and, with wire whisk, beat in molasses and 1 cup sugar until blended; whisk in egg. With wooden spoon, stir in flour, baking soda, cinnamon, ginger, salt, and cloves until mixed. Transfer dough to medium bowl and freeze until firm enough to handle, about 15 minutes.

3 Spread remaining ¼ cup sugar on sheet of waxed paper. With hands, shape dough into 1-inch balls; roll balls in sugar to coat. Place balls, 2½ inches apart, on ungreased large cookie sheet. Bake until cookies spread and darken, 10 to 12 minutes. Cool on cookie sheet on wire rack 1 minute. With wide metal spatula, transfer cookies to rack to cool completely. Repeat with remaining dough and sugar.

4 Store cookies in cookie jar up to 1 week.

each cookie About 45 calories, 1g protein, 7g carbohydrate, 2g total fat (0g saturated), 0g fiber, 3mg cholesterol, 75mg sodium

Melt-in-Your-Mouth Sugar Cookies

With vegetable oil substituting in for some of the butter, this recipe gives you all the rich crispness without the saturated fat.

active time 40 minutes *bake time* 10 to 11 minutes per batch *makes* 96 cookies

2¼ cups all-purpose flour
½ teaspoon baking soda
½ teaspoon cream of tartar
¼ teaspoon salt
½ cup butter (1 stick), softened (no substitutions)
½ cup confectioners' sugar
½ cup plus 2 tablespoons granulated sugar
1 large egg
½ cup vegetable oil
1 teaspoon vanilla extract

1 Preheat oven to 350°F. On waxed paper, combine flour, baking soda, cream of tartar, and salt.

2 In large bowl, with mixer on medium speed, beat butter, confectioners' sugar, and ½ cup granulated sugar until creamy, 2 minutes. On low speed, beat in egg, then oil and vanilla. Gradually beat in flour mixture just until blended, occasionally scraping bowl with rubber spatula.

3 Place remaining 2 tablespoons granulated sugar in saucer. With hands, shape dough by rounded measuring teaspoons into ¾-inch balls. Place balls, 2 inches apart, on ungreased large cookie sheet. Dip punch cup or glass with raised or cut design on bottom, or coarse side of meat mallet, into sugar in saucer; use to press and flatten each ball into 1½-inch round.

4 Bake until edges are golden, 10 to 11 minutes. With wide metal spatula, transfer cookies to wire rack to cool. Repeat with remaining dough and granulated sugar.

5 Store cookies in cookie jar up to 1 week.

each cookie About 40 calories, 0g protein, 4g carbohydrate, 2g total fat (1g saturated), 0g fiber, 5mg cholesterol, 25mg sodium

Walnut Balls

These buttery mouthfuls are a traditional choice for the holiday cookie jar.

active time 45 minutes   *bake time* 13 to 15 minutes per batch   *makes* 78 cookies

1 cup butter (2 sticks), softened (no substitutions)
6 tablespoons granulated sugar
½ teaspoon vanilla extract
2 cups all-purpose flour
⅛ teaspoon salt
2 cups walnuts (8 ounces), chopped
1¼ cups confectioners' sugar

1   Preheat oven to 325°F.

2   In large bowl, with mixer on medium speed, beat butter, granulated sugar, and vanilla until creamy, occasionally scraping bowl with rubber spatula. On low speed, gradually beat in flour and salt just until blended, occasionally scraping bowl. Stir in walnuts.

3   With hands, shape dough by rounded measuring teaspoons into 1-inch balls. Place balls, 1 inch apart, on ungreased large cookie sheet. Bake until bottoms are lightly browned, 13 to 15 minutes.

4   Place confectioners' sugar in pie plate. While cookies are hot, with wide metal spatula, transfer 4 or 5 cookies at a time to pie plate with confectioners' sugar. Gently turn cookies with fork to generously coat with sugar. Transfer to wire rack to cool completely. Repeat with remaining dough and confectioners' sugar.

5   Store cookies in cookie jar up to 1 week.

each cookie About 65 calories, 1g protein, 6g carbohydrate, 4g total fat (2g saturated), 0g fiber, 7mg cholesterol, 30mg sodium

Honey Cookies

These slightly salty cookies are perfect for those who prefer their treats not too sweet.

active time 40 minutes plus chilling   *bake time* 18 to 22 minutes per batch
makes 36 cookies

- 1 cup butter or margarine (2 sticks), softened
- ¼ cup honey (see Tip)
- 2 teaspoons vanilla extract
- 2 cups all-purpose flour
- 2 cups walnuts (8 ounces), chopped
- ½ teaspoon salt

1 In large bowl, with mixer on high speed, beat butter until creamy. Add honey and vanilla; beat until well blended. On low speed, beat in flour, walnuts, and salt until dough forms. Cover bowl with plastic wrap and refrigerate 1 hour.

2 Preheat oven to 325°F. With lightly floured hands, shape dough by heaping measuring teaspoons into ½-inch balls. Place balls, 2 inches apart, on ungreased large cookie sheet. Press floured four-tine fork across top of each ball (page 23). Bake until golden, 18 to 22 minutes. With wide metal spatula, transfer cookies to wire rack to cool. Repeat with remaining dough.

3 Store cookies in cookie jar up to 1 week.

each cookie About 105 calories, 1g protein, 7g carbohydrate, 8g total fat (1g saturated), 1g fiber, 0mg cholesterol, 85mg sodium

cookie tip In general, the darker the color of a honey the stronger the flavor. Choose a light delicate variety, such as orange blossom honey, for these cookies.

Wheat-Free Almond Butter Cookies

Here's a sweet treat for cookie lovers who are intolerant of both dairy and gluten. You can find flaxseeds and almond butter in natural food stores.

active time 10 minutes *bake time* 11 to 12 minutes per batch *makes* 36 cookies

1 tablespoon ground flaxseeds or flaxseed meal
3 tablespoons water
1 cup smooth almond butter
1 cup packed brown sugar
1 teaspoon baking soda
½ teaspoon vanilla extract
  pinch salt
½ teaspoon pumpkin pie spice (optional)
  sliced almonds (optional)

1 Preheat oven to 350°F. Line two large cookie sheets with parchment paper.

2 In small bowl, mix flaxseeds with water. Let stand 5 minutes.

3 In a large bowl, with mixer on low speed, blend almond butter, brown sugar, baking soda, vanilla, salt, soaked flaxseeds, and pumpkin pie spice if using until thoroughly combined.

4 With hands, shape dough by rounded measuring tablespoons into ¾-inch balls. Place balls, 1½ inches apart, on prepared cookie sheets. If desired, top balls with almonds. Bake until slightly golden, 11 to 12 minutes. Using wide metal spatula, transfer cookies to wire rack to cool. Repeat with remaining dough.

5 Store cookies in a cookie jar up to 3 days.

each serving About 70 calories, 1g protein, 8g carbohydrate, 4g total fat (0.5g saturated), 13g fiber, 0mg cholesterol, 72mg sodium

cookie tip When you organize your cookie platters for a Christmas party, group your gluten-free and lower-calorie offerings together and place printed cards nearby to let your guests know where to find them.

Hermits

Originating in New England's clipper-ship days, these spicy fruit cookies got their name from their long-keeping quality.

active time 20 minutes   *bake time* 13 to 15 minutes   *makes* 32 cookies

2 cups all-purpose flour
1 teaspoon ground cinnamon
½ teaspoon baking powder
½ teaspoon baking soda
½ teaspoon ground ginger
¼ teaspoon ground nutmeg
¼ teaspoon salt
⅛ teaspoon ground cloves
1 cup packed brown sugar
½ cup butter or margarine (1 stick), softened
⅓ cup dark molasses
1 large egg
1 cup dark seedless raisins
1 cup pecans (optional), toasted (page 33) and coarsely chopped

1 Preheat oven to 350°F. Grease and flour two large cookie sheets.

2 On sheet of waxed paper, combine flour, cinnamon, baking powder, baking soda, ginger, nutmeg, salt, and cloves.

3 In large bowl, with mixer on medium speed, beat brown sugar and butter until light and fluffy. Beat in molasses until well combined. Beat in egg. With mixer on low speed, beat in flour mixture just until blended, occasionally scraping bowl with rubber spatula. With spoon, stir in raisins and pecans, if using.

4 Divide dough into quarters. With lightly floured hands, shape each quarter into 12″ by 1½″ log. On each prepared cookie sheet, place two logs, leaving 3 inches in between. Bake until logs flatten and edges are firm, 13 to 15 minutes, rotating cookie sheets between upper and lower oven racks halfway through baking. Cool logs on cookie sheets on wire racks 15 minutes.

5 Transfer logs to cutting board. Slice each crosswise into 8 cookies. Using wide metal spatula, transfer to racks to cool completely.

6 Store cookies in cookie jar up to 3 weeks.

each cookie About 105 calories, 1g protein, 19g carbohydrate, 3g total fat (2g saturated), 0g fiber, 15mg cholesterol, 80mg sodium

Best Linzer Cookies

Freezing the dough helps the cookies stay well defined while baking. Freeze for 10 minutes after rolling, and another 10 minutes after cutting.

active time 2 hours plus chilling *bake time* 17 to 20 minutes per batch
makes 96 cookies

- 2 **bags (8 ounces each) pecans**
- 1 **cup cornstarch**
- 3 **cups butter (6 sticks), softened (no substitutions)**
- 2⅔ **cups confectioners' sugar**
- 4 **teaspoons vanilla extract**
- 1½ **teaspoons salt**
- 2 **large eggs**
- 5½ **cups all-purpose flour**
- 1½ **cups seedless raspberry jam**

1 In a food processor with knife blade attached, pulse pecans and cornstarch until pecans are finely ground.

2 In a large bowl, with mixer at low speed, beat butter and 2 cups confectioners' sugar until blended. Increase speed to high; beat until light and fluffy, about 3 minutes, scraping bowl with rubber spatula. At medium speed, beat in vanilla, salt, and eggs. On low speed, gradually beat in flour and pecan mixture just until blended, scraping bowl.

3 Divide dough into 8 equal pieces; flatten each piece into a disk and wrap in plastic wrap. Refrigerate until dough is firm enough to roll, 4 to 5 hours.

4 Preheat oven to 325°F. Remove 1 disk of dough from refrigerator; let stand 5 minutes for easier rolling. On floured surface, with floured rolling pin, roll dough ⅛ inch thick. With floured 2¼-inch fluted square cookie cutter, cut dough into as many cookies as possible. With floured 1¾-inch star cutter, cut out centers from half of cookies. With spatula, place cookies 1 inch apart on ungreased cookie sheets. Repeat with remaining dough and trimmings.

5 Bake cookies until edges are golden, 17 to 20 minutes. Transfer cookies to wire rack to cool. Repeat with remaining dough and trimmings.

6 Sprinkle remaining $2/3$ cup confectioners' sugar through sieve over cooled cookies with cut-out centers.

7 In a small bowl, stir jam until smooth. Spread top of each whole cookie with scant teaspoon jam; place cut-out cookies on top. Store in tightly sealed container, with waxed paper between layers, at room temperature up to 1 week or in freezer up to 2 months. (If cookies are stored in freezer, re-sprinkle with confectioners' sugar before serving.)

each cookie About 115 calories, 1g protein, 11g carbohydrate, 8g total fat (3g saturated), 1g fiber, 17mg cholesterol, 80mg sodium

cookie tip You can replace the raspberry preserves with your favorite flavor of preserves; just make sure they are seedless. Lemon curd or chocolate-hazelnut spread would also be delicious alternatives.

Mandelbrot

An Eastern European cookie, mandelbrot, or almond bread, is baked in logs, sliced, and rebaked just like biscotti.

active time 30 minutes plus cooling *bake time* 37 to 38 minutes
makes 48 cookies

3¾ cups all-purpose flour
2 teaspoons baking powder
½ teaspoon salt
3 large eggs
1 cup sugar
¾ cup vegetable oil
2 teaspoons vanilla extract
¼ teaspoon almond extract
1 teaspoon freshly grated orange peel
1 cup blanched almonds (4 ounces), coarsely chopped and toasted (page 33) until golden

1 Preheat oven to 350°F. In large bowl, stir together flour, baking powder, and salt.

2 In separate large bowl, with mixer on medium speed, beat eggs and sugar until mixture is light lemon color. Add oil, vanilla and almond extracts, and orange peel and beat until blended. With wooden spoon, beat in flour mixture. Stir in almonds.

3 Divide dough in half. Drop each half by spoonfuls down length of ungreased large cookie sheet. With lightly floured hands, shape each half into 12-inch-long log, leaving 4 inches between logs (dough will be slightly sticky). Bake until lightly colored and firm, 30 minutes. Cool logs on cookie sheet on wire rack 10 minutes.

4 Transfer logs to cutting board. With serrated knife, cut each log crosswise into ½-inch-thick slices. Place slices, cut side down, on two ungreased large cookie sheets. Bake until golden, 7 to 8 minutes, turning slices over and rotating cookie sheets halfway through baking. With wide metal spatula, transfer cookies to racks to cool completely.

5 Store cookies in cookie jar up to 3 weeks.

each cookie About 105 calories, 2g protein, 12g carbohydrate, 5g total fat (1g saturated), 0.5g fiber, 13mg cholesterol, 50mg sodium

Triple-Nut Biscotti

It's a triple dose of nuttiness with the added zing of fresh lemon peel.

active time 25 minutes plus cooling *bake time* 45 minutes *makes* 48 biscotti

⅓ cup whole natural almonds
⅓ cup shelled pistachios
⅓ cup walnuts
1 cup all-purpose flour
⅔ cup whole-wheat flour
⅔ cup sugar
¼ cup toasted wheat germ
1½ teaspoons baking powder
½ teaspoon ground cinnamon
¼ teaspoon salt
2 large egg whites
1 large egg
¼ cup water
½ teaspoon freshly grated lemon peel

1 Preheat oven to 325°F. Grease large cookie sheet.

2 In 13" by 9" baking pan, bake nuts until toasted, about 15 minutes, stirring once. Cool in pan on wire rack. Coarsely chop nuts.

3 In large bowl, stir nuts, flours, sugar, wheat germ, baking powder, cinnamon, and salt until well mixed. In small bowl, beat egg whites, egg, water, and lemon peel. Stir egg mixture into nut mixture, then, with floured hands, press dough just until blended.

4 Divide dough in half. On prepared cookie sheet, with floured hands, shape each half into 9-inch log, placing logs 3 inches apart (dough will be sticky). Bake 35 minutes or until toothpick inserted in center comes out clean. Cool logs on cookie sheet on rack 30 minutes.

5 Transfer 1 log to cutting board. With serrated knife, cut crosswise on diagonal into ¼-inch-thick slices. Place slices, cut side down, on ungreased large cookie sheet. Repeat with remaining log, using second cookie sheet if necessary. Bake 15 minutes or until golden, rotating cookie sheets between upper and lower oven racks halfway through baking. Using wide metal spatula, transfer biscotti to rack to cool.

6 Store biscotti in cookie jar up to 3 weeks.

each biscotto About 45 calories, 2g protein, 7g carbohydrate, 2g total fat (0g saturated), 1g fiber, 4mg cholesterol, 30mg sodium

Cherry and Ginger Biscotti

These biscotti are a taste surprise, with the chewy tartness of dried cherries and the hot, bright flavor of crystallized ginger. Or, if you prefer a more traditional biscotti, try the almond variation, which substitutes toasted almonds and amaretto liqueur for the ginger and cherries.

active time 35 minutes plus cooling *bake time* 50 to 60 minutes
makes 54 biscotti

3¼ cups all-purpose flour
 1 tablespoon baking powder
 1 teaspoon ground ginger
 ½ teaspoon salt
 ¾ cup butter or margarine (1½ sticks), cut up
1¼ cups sugar
 3 large eggs
 1 jar (2 ounces) diced crystallized ginger (⅓ cup), coarsely chopped
 ¾ cup dried tart cherries, chopped

1 Preheat oven to 350°F. On waxed paper, combine flour, baking powder, ground ginger, and salt.

2 In microwave-safe large bowl, heat butter in microwave oven on High 1 minute or until butter melts. With wire whisk, mix in sugar and eggs until smooth. With spoon, stir flour mixture, crystallized ginger, and cherries into egg mixture until dough forms.

3 Divide dough in half. On ungreased large cookie sheet, with floured hands, shape 1 half into 14″ by 4″ log (about ½ inch high). Repeat with remaining dough on second cookie sheet. Bake until golden and toothpick inserted in center comes out clean, 25 to 30 minutes, rotating cookie sheets between upper and lower oven racks halfway through baking. Cool biscotti on cookie sheets on wire racks 20 minutes. Reset oven to 325°F.

4 Transfer 1 log to cutting board. With serrated knife, cut crosswise into ½-inch-thick slices. Place slices, cut side down, on same cookie sheets. Repeat with remaining

log. Bake until golden on bottom, 25 to 30 minutes, rotating cookie sheets between upper and lower oven racks halfway through baking. With wide metal spatula, transfer biscotti to racks to cool completely.

5 Store biscotti in cookie jar up to 3 weeks.

each biscotto About 80 calories, 1g protein, 13g carbohydrate, 3g total fat (2g saturated), 0g fiber, 19mg cholesterol, 75mg sodium

almond biscotti

Prepare as directed, but omit ground ginger, add **2 tablespoons amaretto (almond-flavor liqueur)** to egg mixture, and substitute **1½ cups sliced almonds (6 ounces),** lightly toasted (page 33) and cooled, for crystallized ginger and cherries. Store in cookie jar up to 3 weeks.

each biscotto About 95 calories, 2g protein, 11g carbohydrate, 5g total fat (2g saturated), 1g fiber, 19mg cholesterol, 75mg sodium

Crunchy Low-Fat Chocolate Biscotti

We've given this biscotti recipe a healthy makeover, using egg whites instead of whole eggs and vegetable oil instead of butter.

active time 30 minutes plus cooling *bake time* 50 minutes *makes* 48 biscotti

- 3 large egg whites
- ⅓ cup vegetable oil
- 2 tablespoons strong brewed coffee
- 1 teaspoon vanilla extract
- 1⅔ cups all-purpose flour
- ¾ cup sugar
- ½ cup unsweetened cocoa
- 1 teaspoon baking powder
- ¼ teaspoon baking soda
- ¼ teaspoon salt
- ⅓ cup chopped hazelnuts or other nuts, toasted (page 33)
- ⅓ cup dried tart cherries

1 Preheat oven to 350°F. Lightly grease large cookie sheet.

2 In small bowl, beat together egg whites, oil, coffee, and vanilla.

3 In large bowl, stir together flour, sugar, cocoa, baking powder, baking soda, salt, nuts, and cherries until well mixed. Pour egg mixture over dry ingredients and stir until combined. Shape dough into two 12" by 1" logs; place both on prepared cookie sheet and flatten slightly. Bake 30 minutes or until toothpick inserted in center comes out clean. Cool logs on cookie sheet on wire rack 10 minutes.

4 Transfer 1 log to cutting board. Cut diagonally into scant ½-inch-thick slices. Arrange biscotti, cut side up, on ungreased cookie sheet. Repeat with remaining log, using a second cookie sheet if necessary. Bake 20 minutes until dry. Rotate cookie sheets between upper and lower oven racks halfway though baking, if using two sheets. Using wide metal spatula, transfer biscotti to rack to cool.

5 Store biscotti in cookie jar up to 3 weeks.

each biscotto About 50 calories, 1g protein, 8g carbohydrate, 2g total fat (1g saturated), 1g fiber, 0mg cholesterol, 30mg sodium

Icebox Cookies

Icebox (or refrigerator) cookies bring back memories of childhood, whether our moms baked us this kind of cookie or not. Icebox cookies became the rage—and an early convenience food—in the late nineteenth century, when women discovered that having a roll of cookie dough in the icebox meant they could bake and serve warm cookies at a moment's notice. This time saver is just as useful today.

A number of the recipes in this chapter yield a lot of cookies. If you like, you can cut the recipe in half, but we suggest that you make the full recipe and simply stash the extra dough in the freezer for cookies in a flash.

Basic Cookie Dough (recipe page 84) and
Gingerbread Cutouts (recipe page 87)

Here are a few tips for icebox cookie success every time:

If the dough seems too soft to shape into a log or rectangle, as directed, put it in the refrigerator for 15 minutes or so to firm it up.

If you take the option to use margarine instead of butter, freeze the dough instead of refrigerating it to firm it up.

If the recipe directs you to shape the dough into a log, check on it every 10 minutes or so, once it's in the refrigerator (or freezer). While it's still soft, the weight of the dough may cause the log to start to flatten on one side. If this happens, roll it back and forth to reshape it. Continue to do this until the dough is firm enough to keep the shape you need.

To freeze dough for icebox cookies, wrap it tightly in heavy-duty foil and pack it in an airtight container. Label it with the date. Let the dough thaw in the refrigerator before slicing and baking.

When slicing a rounded log of dough (as opposed to one that's squared off), turn it every few slices to keep the bottom from flattening.

Garden-Party Sugar Cookies

Fresh thyme, lemon peel, and crystallized ginger bring complex flavor to these easy-to-make cookies.

active time 30 minutes plus chilling *bake time* 12 to 14 minutes per batch
makes 96 cookies (48 cookies per log of dough)

2½ cups all-purpose flour
1 teaspoon baking soda
1 teaspoon cream of tartar
½ teaspoon salt
1 cup butter or margarine (2 sticks), softened
2 cups confectioners' sugar, plus additional for sprinkling
1 large egg
1 tablespoon freshly grated lemon peel
1 tablespoon fresh thyme leaves (preferably lemon thyme), minced
1 tablespoon minced crystallized ginger

1 In medium bowl, combine flour, baking soda, cream of tartar, and salt.

2 In large bowl, with mixer on low speed, beat butter and 2 cups confectioners' sugar until blended. Increase speed to high; beat until creamy. On low speed, beat in egg, lemon peel, thyme, and ginger. Beat in flour mixture just until blended.

3 Divide dough in half. Shape each half into 12″ by 1½″ log; wrap each log in plastic wrap (see page 85). Freeze until firm enough to slice, 2 hours, or up to 1 month.

4 Preheat oven to 350°F. Cut 1 log crosswise into ¼-inch-thick slices. Place slices, 1 inch apart, on ungreased large cookie sheet. Bake until edges are golden brown, 12 to 14 minutes. With wide metal spatula, transfer cookies to wire rack to cool. Repeat with remaining dough.

5 When cookies are cool, sprinkle lightly with confectioners' sugar. Store in cookie jar up to 1 week.

each cookie About 40 calories, 0g protein, 5g carbohydrate, 2g total fat (0g saturated), 0g fiber, 2mg cholesterol, 50mg sodium

Basic Cookie Dough

You can use this dough to make Christmas cookies in any shape you choose, including the candy canes and Christmas trees featured on our cover. Get creative with various sizes of decorating tips, as well as different colors.

active time 30 minutes plus chilling *bake time* 10 to 12 minutes per batch
makes 60 cookies

Basic Cookie Dough
- 1 cup (2 sticks) butter (no substitutions), softened
- ½ cup sugar
- 1 large egg
- 1 tablespoon vanilla extract
- 3 cups all-purpose flour
- ½ teaspoon baking powder
  Ornamental Frosting (optional)

Ornamental Frosting
- 1 package (16 ounces) confectioners' sugar
- 3 tablespoons meringue powder
- ⅓ cup warm water
  assorted food colorings

1 In large bowl, with mixer at low speed, beat butter and sugar until blended. Increase speed to high; beat until light and creamy. At low speed, beat in egg and vanilla. Beat in flour and baking powder just until blended.

2 Divide dough into 4 equal pieces. Wrap each piece with plastic wrap and refrigerate 1 hour or until dough is firm enough to roll. (Or place dough in freezer for 30 minutes.)

3 Preheat oven to 350°F. On a lightly floured surface, with floured rolling pin, roll 1 piece of dough ⅛ inch thick. With floured 3- to 4-inch assorted cookie cutters, cut dough into as many cookies as possible; wrap and refrigerate trimmings. Place cookies, 1 inch apart, on ungreased large cookie sheet.

4 Bake cookies 10 to 12 minutes or until lightly browned. Transfer cookies to wire rack to cool. Repeat with remaining dough and trimmings.

5 When cookies are cool, prepare Ornamental Frosting (if you like): In bowl, with mixer at medium speed, beat confectioners' sugar, meringue powder, and water until blended and mixture is so stiff that knife drawn through it leaves a clean-cut path, about 5 minutes. Tint frosting with food colorings as desired; keep surface covered with plastic to prevent drying out. Use frosting to decorate cookies as desired. Set cookies aside to allow frosting to dry completely, about 1 hour.

6 Store cookies in a tightly covered container (with waxed paper between layers, if decorated) at room temperature up to 2 weeks, or in freezer up to 3 months.

each cookie About 75 calories, 1g protein, 11g carbohydrate, 3g total fat (2g saturated), 0g fiber, 12mg cholesterol, 50mg sodium

cookie tip

When packaging cookies as a gift, wrap them in pairs, placing the flat bottoms together, and wrap in foil, plastic wrap, or cellophane bags.

shaping & slicing icebox cookies

step 1: Shape dough roughly into a log, then use plastic wrap or waxed paper to roll and smooth it into a cylinder of even thickness.

step 2: As you slice the log of dough, turn it every few cuts so the bottom doesn't become flattened.

Lime Slice-'n'-Bakes

The refreshing flavor of lime creates a delicate cookie. Shaping the dough into rectangles before chilling makes it easier to slice the cookies because the dough rests flat on the cutting board and doesn't lose its shape from the pressure of the knife.

active time 30 minutes plus chilling *bake time* 12 to 15 minutes per batch *makes* 48 cookies (24 cookies per brick of dough)

3 limes
½ cup butter or margarine (1 stick), softened
¾ cup granulated sugar
1 large egg
1¾ cups all-purpose flour
½ cup confectioners' sugar

1 From limes, grate 1 teaspoon peel and squeeze 3 tablespoons juice (see page 39 for tips). In medium bowl, with mixer on medium speed, beat butter and granulated sugar until creamy. On low speed, beat in egg and lime peel and juice until blended. Beat in flour until combined.

2 Divide dough in half. On separate sheets of plastic wrap, shape each half into 6" by 2½" by 1½" brick. Wrap each brick in plastic and freeze 3 hours or up to 1 month.

3 Preheat oven to 350°F. Slice 1 brick crosswise into ¼-inch-thick slices. Place slices, 1 inch apart, on ungreased large cookie sheet. Bake until edges are golden brown, 12 to 15 minutes. With wide metal spatula, transfer cookies to wire racks. Sift confectioners' sugar over hot cookies. Repeat with remaining dough and confectioners' sugar.

4 Store cookies in cookie jar up to 1 week.

each cookie About 50 calories, 1g protein, 8g carbohydrate, 2g total fat (1g saturated), 0g fiber, 10mg cholesterol, 20mg sodium

Gingerbread Cutouts

For these snappy Gingerbread Cutouts, combine Basic Cookie Dough (page 84) with molasses, nutmeg, cloves, and ginger.

active time 30 minutes plus chilling *bake time* 11 to 13 minutes per batch
makes 60 cookies

Basic Cookie Dough
(page 84)
½ teaspoon baking soda
2 teaspoons ground
cinnamon
2 teaspoons ground ginger
½ teaspoon ground nutmeg
¼ teaspoon ground cloves
¾ cup packed dark brown
sugar
¼ cup dark molasses
Ornamental Frosting
(page 84; optional)
decorative candies
(optional)

1 Prepare Basic Cookie Dough, but in step 1, add baking soda and spices to flour mixture. Reduce butter to 1 stick, substitute dark brown sugar for granulated, and add molasses with egg and vanilla.

2 Divide dough into 3 equal pieces. Flatten each into a disk; wrap each in plastic wrap. Refrigerate dough 2 hours or overnight.

3 Preheat oven to 350°F. Between 2 sheets of waxed paper, roll 1 disk of dough ⅛ inch thick. Remove top sheet of waxed paper. With floured 3- to 4-inch shaped cookie cutters, cut out as many cookies as possible; wrap and refrigerate trimmings. Place cookies, 1 inch apart, on ungreased large cookie sheet.

4 Bake cookies 11 to 13 minutes or until edges begin to brown. Transfer cookies to wire rack to cool. Repeat with remaining dough.

5 When cookies are cool, prepare Ornamental Frosting (if you like); add candies to decorate. Set cookies aside to allow frosting to dry.

6 Store cookies (putting sheets of waxed paper between layers if decorated) in tightly sealed container at room temperature up to 2 weeks or in freezer up to 2 months.

each cookie About 75 calories, 1g protein, 11g carbohydrate, 3g total fat (2g saturated), 0g fiber, 12mg cholesterol, 50mg sodium

Butterscotch Fingers

When butter and brown sugar are combined, they are magically transformed into the treat we know as butterscotch.

active time 30 minutes plus chilling *bake time* 12 to 14 minutes per batch
makes 66 cookies

2⅓ cups all-purpose flour
½ teaspoon baking powder
½ teaspoon salt
1 cup butter or margarine (2 sticks), softened
1 cup packed dark brown sugar
1 teaspoon vanilla extract
1 large egg
¾ cup pecans, chopped

1 On waxed paper, combine flour, baking powder, and salt.

2 In large bowl, with mixer on medium speed, beat butter and brown sugar until creamy, occasionally scraping bowl with rubber spatula. Beat in vanilla, then egg. On low speed, gradually add flour mixture; beat just until blended, occasionally scraping bowl. With spoon, stir in pecans.

3 Shape dough into 12" by 3¾" by 1" brick. Wrap in plastic and refrigerate until firm enough to slice, 6 hours or overnight; if using margarine, freeze overnight. (Dough can also be frozen up to 3 months.)

4 Preheat oven to 350°F. Grease large cookie sheet.

5 With sharp knife, cut brick crosswise into ⅛-inch-thick slices. Place slices, 1 inch apart, on prepared cookie sheet. Bake until lightly browned around edges, 12 to 14 minutes. With wide metal spatula, transfer to wire rack to cool. Repeat with remaining dough.

6 Store cookies in cookie jar up to 1 week.

each cookie About 65 calories, 1g protein, 7g carbohydrate, 4g total fat (2g saturated), 0g fiber, 11mg cholesterol, 55mg sodium

Maple Pecan Cookies

Dark brown sugar, maple extract, and pecans make a deeply flavored cookie; cake flour yields a tender crumb.

active time 25 minutes plus chilling *bake time* 18 to 20 minutes per batch
makes 84 cookies (21 cookies per log of dough)

- 4 cups cake flour (not self-rising)
- 1 teaspoon baking powder
- 1 teaspoon baking soda
- ½ teaspoon salt
- 3 cups packed dark brown sugar
- 1 cup butter or margarine (2 sticks), softened
- 2 large eggs
- 2 teaspoons natural maple extract or imitation maple flavor (see Tip)
- 1 package (7 ounces) sweetened flaked coconut (2⅔ cups)
- 1 cup pecans (4 ounces), chopped

1 On waxed paper, combine flour, baking powder, baking soda, and salt.

2 In large bowl, with mixer on medium speed, beat brown sugar and butter until creamy, occasionally scraping bowl with rubber spatula. On low speed, beat in eggs and maple extract. Gradually beat in flour mixture until blended. Stir in coconut and pecans.

3 Divide dough into 4 equal pieces. Shape each piece into 9" by 2" log. Roll each log in plastic wrap (see page 85). Refrigerate until dough is firm enough to slice, 3 hours or overnight; if using margarine, freeze 4 hours. (Dough can also be frozen up to 3 months.)

4 Preheat oven to 350°F. Cut 1 log into scant ½-inch-thick slices. Place slices, 1 inch apart, on ungreased large cookie sheet. Bake until firm and edges brown slightly, 18 to 20 minutes. Using wide metal spatula, transfer cookies to wire rack to cool. Repeat with remaining dough.

5 Store cookies in cookie jar up to 2 weeks.

each cookie About 90 calories, 1g protein, 13g carbohydrate, 4g total fat (2g saturated), 0g fiber, 11mg cholesterol, 60mg sodium

cookie tip Be sure to use maple extract and not maple syrup; you'll find it in the baking aisle of the supermarket.

Oatmeal Icebox Cookies

These crisp oatmeal slices are the perfect after-school treat.

active time 35 minutes plus chilling *bake time* 14 minutes per batch
makes 60 cookies (30 cookies per log of dough)

1½ cups all-purpose flour
 1 teaspoon baking powder
 ½ teaspoon baking soda
 ¼ teaspoon salt
 1 cup butter or margarine
   (2 sticks), softened
 1 cup packed dark brown
   sugar
 ¾ cup granulated sugar
 2 large eggs
 2 teaspoons vanilla extract
 3 cups old-fashioned oats,
   uncooked
 1 cup pecans (4 ounces)
 1 cup dark seedless raisins

1 On waxed paper, stir together flour, baking powder, baking soda, and salt until blended.

2 In large bowl, with mixer on medium speed, beat butter and sugars until creamy, occasionally scraping bowl with rubber spatula. Beat in eggs, one at a time, until blended. Beat in vanilla. On low speed, beat in flour mixture until combined. With wooden spoon, stir in oats, pecans, and raisins.

3 Divide dough in half. On separate sheets of plastic wrap, shape each half into 12-inch-long log. Roll each log in plastic wrap (see page 85). Refrigerate until firm, 4 hours or overnight; if using margarine, freeze 4 hours. (Dough can also be frozen up to 3 months.)

4 Preheat oven to 350°F. With serrated knife, using sawing motion, cut 1 log crosswise into ⅜-inch-thick slices. Place slices, 2 inches apart, on two ungreased large cookie sheets. Bake until golden brown, 14 minutes, rotating cookie sheets between upper and lower oven racks halfway through baking. Cool cookies on cookie sheets on wire racks 2 minutes. With wide metal spatula, transfer cookies to racks to cool completely.

5 Store cookies in cookie jar up to 1 week.

each cookie About 100 calories, 1g protein, 13g carbohydrate, 5g total fat (2g saturated), 0.5g fiber, 15mg cholesterol, 65mg sodium

Almond Slices

These thin, crispy cookies are almond heaven.

active time 25 minutes plus chilling *bake time* 10 minutes per batch
makes 84 cookies (42 cookies per brick of dough)

1¾ cups sugar
 1 cup butter or margarine (2 sticks), softened
 ¼ cup light (mild) molasses
 1 tablespoon ground ginger
 1 tablespoon vanilla extract
 1 teaspoon baking soda
 1 teaspoon salt
 2 large eggs
 4 cups all-purpose flour
 2 cups sliced almonds

1 In large bowl, with mixer on medium speed, beat sugar, butter, molasses, ginger, vanilla, baking soda, salt, eggs, and 2 cups flour. With wooden spoon, stir in almonds and remaining 2 cups flour; if necessary, use hands to mix thoroughly, as dough will be very stiff.

2 Divide dough in half. Shape each half into 10" by 3" by 1" brick; wrap each brick with plastic wrap. Refrigerate until firm enough to slice, 4 hours or up to 1 week; if using margarine, freeze 4 hours. (Bricks can also be frozen up to 3 months.)

3 Preheat oven to 400°F. Grease large cookie sheet. With serrated knife, cut 1 brick into scant ¼-inch-thick slices. Place slices, 1 inch apart, on prepared cookie sheet. Bake until golden, 10 minutes. With wide metal spatula, transfer cookies to wire rack to cool. Repeat with remaining dough.

4 Store cookies in cookie jar up to 2 weeks.

each cookie About 75 calories, 1g protein, 10g carbohydrate, 3g total fat (1g saturated), 0g fiber, 5mg cholesterol, 70mg sodium

cookie tip Prepare several batches of icebox cookie dough and freeze in logs (see page 85 for instructions). When people drop by or you need cookies for a last-minute party invite, you can quickly bake as few or as many cookies as you need.

Chocolate Pinwheels

Can't decide between chocolate and vanilla? Try these!

active time 30 minutes plus chilling *bake time* 10 to 12 minutes per batch
makes 48 cookies (24 cookies per log of dough)

2¾ cups plus 2 tablespoons all-purpose flour
¼ teaspoon baking soda
¼ teaspoon salt
1 cup butter (2 sticks), softened (do not use margarine)
¾ cup granulated sugar
1 large egg
1 teaspoon vanilla extract
⅓ cup miniature semisweet chocolate chips
¼ cup confectioners' sugar
1 square (1 ounce) unsweetened chocolate, melted
2 tablespoons unsweetened cocoa

1 On waxed paper, combine 2¾ cups flour, baking soda, and salt.

2 In large bowl, with mixer on medium speed, beat butter and granulated sugar until creamy. Add egg and vanilla; beat until well mixed. On low speed, beat in flour mixture.

3 Divide dough in half. Stir chocolate chips, confectioners' sugar, melted chocolate, and cocoa into one half. Stir remaining 2 tablespoons flour into plain dough half.

4 On waxed paper, roll chocolate dough into 14" by 10" rectangle. Repeat with plain dough. Leaving plain rectangle on waxed paper, pick up and place it, dough side down, evenly on top of chocolate rectangle. Peel off top sheet of waxed paper. Starting from long side, tightly roll dough, jelly-roll fashion, to form log, lifting bottom sheet of waxed paper to help roll. Cut log crosswise in half. Wrap each half, freeze 2 hours or refrigerate overnight.

5 Preheat oven to 350°F. Cut 1 log crosswise into ¼-inch-thick slices. Place slices, 2 inches apart, on two ungreased cookie sheets. Bake until lightly browned, 10 to 12 minutes. With spatula, transfer cookies to wire rack to cool. Repeat with second log.

6 Store cookies in cookie jar up to 1 week.

each cookie About 90 calories, 1g protein, 10g carbohydrate, 5g total fat (3g saturated), 0g fiber, 16mg cholesterol, 60mg sodium

Checkerboard Cookies

Chocolate and vanilla make up the tasty checkerboard design of these refrigerator squares. The secret is to glue the dough pieces together with milk before chilling them. For step-by-step photos, see Forming & Slicing Checkerboard Dough, opposite.

active time 40 minutes plus chilling *bake time* 10 minutes per batch
makes 48 cookies

2 cups all-purpose flour
1 teaspoon baking powder
¼ teaspoon salt
½ cup (1 stick) plus 1 tablespoon butter or margarine, softened
1 cup sugar
1 large egg
1 teaspoon vanilla extract
1 square (1 ounce) semisweet chocolate
3 tablespoons unsweetened cocoa
milk for assembling cookies

1 In medium bowl, combine flour, baking powder, and salt. In large bowl, with mixer at medium speed, beat ½ cup butter and sugar until creamy. Reduce speed to low and beat in egg and vanilla until blended. Beat in flour mixture until combined, scraping bowl occasionally with rubber spatula. Remove half of dough; set aside.

2 In 1-quart saucepan, melt chocolate and remaining 1 tablespoon butter over very low heat. Stir in cocoa until combined. Add chocolate mixture to dough in bowl, stirring until thoroughly blended.

3 Separately shape chocolate and vanilla doughs into 12″ by 2″ by 1″ blocks. Slice each block lengthwise into two 12″ by 1″ by 1″ strips. Brush one side of 1 chocolate strip with milk; place brushed side next to 1 vanilla strip. Repeat with remaining 2 strips. Brush top of one vanilla/chocolate rectangle with milk. Place second vanilla/chocolate rectangle on top, reversing colors so end forms checkerboard. Wrap block in waxed paper, using paper to square edges. Refrigerate 4 hours or overnight. (If using margarine, freeze overnight.)

4   Preheat oven to 375°F. Grease two large cookie sheets. Cut dough into ¼-inch-thick slices. Place slices, ½-inch apart, on prepared cookie sheets. Bake until golden, 10 to 12 minutes, rotating cookie sheets between upper and lower racks halfway through baking. Cool on cookie sheets on wire racks 5 minutes. With wide metal spatula, transfer to wire racks to cool completely.

5   Store cookies in cookie jar up to 2 weeks.

each cookie About 60 calories, 1g protein, 9g carbohydrate, 2g total fat (1g saturated), 0g fiber, 10mg cholesterol, 45mg sodium

forming & slicing checkerboard dough

step 1: Cut each 12" by 2" by 1" block of dough in half lengthwise to make two strips.

step 2: After dough has been assembled and chilled, slice it into ¼-inch-thick checkerboard cookies.

Cranberry-Orange Spice Cookies

Crystallized ginger and pumpkin pie spice give these cookies a cold-weather zing that will warm cookie-lovers' hearts.

active time 40 minutes plus chilling *bake time* 14 to 16 minutes per batch
makes 60 cookies (30 cookies per log of dough)

2¾ cups all-purpose flour
¼ teaspoon baking soda
¼ teaspoon salt
1 cup butter (2 sticks), softened (do not use margarine)
¾ cup granulated sugar
1 large egg
1 teaspoon vanilla extract
½ cup dried cranberries, finely chopped
¼ cup crystallized ginger, finely chopped
2 teaspoons freshly grated orange peel
1 teaspoon pumpkin pie spice
3 tablespoons green sugar crystals
3 tablespoons red sugar crystals

1 On waxed paper, combine flour, baking soda, and salt.

2 In large bowl, with mixer on medium speed, beat butter and granulated sugar until creamy, occasionally scraping bowl with rubber spatula. Add egg and vanilla; beat until well mixed. Stir in flour mixture, cranberries, ginger, orange peel, and pumpkin pie spice until well mixed, occasionally scraping bowl. Divide dough in half.

3 On lightly floured surface, with hands, shape each half into 10-inch-long log. Using hands or two clean rulers, press each log to square off sides. Wrap each half in plastic wrap and freeze until firm enough to slice, 2 hours, or refrigerate overnight. (Logs can be frozen up to 1 month.)

4 Preheat oven to 350°F. On waxed paper, place green sugar. Unwrap 1 log and press sides in sugar to coat. Cut log into ¼-inch-thick slices. Place slices, 1 inch apart, on ungreased large cookie sheet. Bake until golden, 14 to 16 minutes. With wide metal spatula, transfer cookies to wire rack to cool. Repeat with red sugar and second log.

5 Store cookies in cookie jar up to 1 week.

each cookie About 70 calories, 1g protein, 9g carbohydrate, 3g total fat (2g saturated), 0g fiber, 12mg cholesterol, 50mg sodium

Anise Slices

These aromatic cookies are perfect with a cup of tea or coffee.

active time 30 minutes plus chilling *bake time* 12 to 14 minutes per batch
makes 88 cookies (44 cookies per rectangle of dough)

½ cup butter (1 stick), softened (do not use margarine)
¾ cup sugar
1 large egg
½ teaspoon vanilla extract
1¾ cups all-purpose flour
1 tablespoon anise seeds, crushed (see Tip)
½ teaspoon baking powder
¼ teaspoon salt

1 In large bowl, with mixer on medium speed, beat butter and sugar until creamy, occasionally scraping bowl with rubber spatula. On low speed, beat in egg and vanilla until blended. Beat in flour, anise seeds, baking powder, and salt until well combined, occasionally scraping bowl.

2 Divide dough in half. Shape each half into 5½" by 2" rectangle. Wrap each rectangle in plastic wrap and refrigerate until firm enough to slice, 2 hours, or freeze 1 hour. (Dough can also be frozen up to 1 month.)

3 Preheat oven to 350°F. Grease large cookie sheet. With knife, cut 1 rectangle crosswise into scant ⅛-inch-thick slices. Place cookies, 1 inch apart, on prepared cookie sheet. Bake until lightly browned, 12 to 14 minutes. With wide metal spatula, transfer cookies to wire rack to cool. Repeat with remaining dough.

4 Store cookies in cookie jar up to 1 week.

each cookie About 25 calories, 0g protein, 3g carbohydrate, 2g total fat (1g saturated), 1g fiber, 6mg cholesterol, 21mg sodium

cookie tip

It's best to use a mortar and pestle to crush the anise seeds, but if you don't have one, coarsely grind them in a spice grinder or place them in a zip-tight plastic bag and crush with a rolling pin.

Brownies & Bar Cookies

Not every bar cookie is a candidate for the Christmas season. Some are too soft or crumbly, while others have gooey tops that would make for a sticky (though sweet) mess if they were to be set on top of one another. The brownies and bars in this chapter are all sturdy and compact enough to survive a cookie-tin pile-on (though we highly doubt they'll be in there for long!).

Cherry Linzer Bars (recipe page 110)

Here are a few tips for brownie and bar cookie success every time:

Prepare the pan before you start mixing the batter. Some rising occurs as soon as the ingredients are moistened. If you line and grease the pan after making the batter, the mixture might start to swell and be harder to spread evenly.

Always use the size and shape of pan specified (for example, don't substitute an 8-inch for a 9-inch pan or a round pan for a square pan).

Don't overmix the batter, as this will result in tough brownies or bars. Unless a recipe specifies otherwise, after adding the flour, mix the batter just until blended.

To check brownies for doneness, insert a toothpick or wooden skewer in the center. Don't use a metal tester; crumbs won't cling to its smooth surface.

Allow bars to cool completely, then cut them with a chef's knife to avoid jagged edges and broken pieces. Use a gentle sawing motion to avoid squashing the bars.

Almond Thins

These bars deliver both the crunch and heady aroma of almonds through the addition of almond extract and sliced almonds.

active time 30 minutes *bake time* 20 minutes *makes* 48 bars

- 2 cups all-purpose flour
- ¾ cup cold butter or margarine (1½ sticks), cut up
- ⅓ cup plus 2 tablespoons sugar
- 1 large egg, separated
- 1 teaspoon almond extract
- 2 tablespoons water
- ⅛ teaspoon salt
- ¾ cup sliced natural almonds

1 Preheat oven to 375°F.

2 In food processor with knife blade attached, blend flour, butter, and ⅓ cup sugar just until mixture forms coarse crumbs. Add egg yolk, almond extract, and water, and blend until mixture just begins to form a ball (do not overmix).

3 With hands, press dough onto bottom of ungreased 15½″ by 10½″ jelly-roll pan. For easier spreading, place plastic wrap over dough and smooth dough evenly over bottom of pan. (To help make an even layer, use bottom of 8- or 9-inch square baking pan to press dough.) Discard plastic wrap.

4 In cup, with fork, beat egg white and salt; brush some over dough. Top dough with almonds; sprinkle with remaining 2 tablespoons sugar. With knife, gently cut dough lengthwise into 6 strips, then cut each strip crosswise into 8 bars.

5 Bake until golden, 20 minutes. Cool in pan on wire rack 5 minutes. While still warm, cut bars again following cut marks. Cool bars completely in pan. With small metal spatula, carefully remove bars from pan.

6 Store bars in cookie jar up to 1 week.

each bar About 65 calories, 1g protein, 6g carbohydrate, 4g total fat (2g saturated), 0g fiber, 13mg cholesterol, 40mg sodium

Caramel-Nut Brownies

Caramels baked right into rich chocolate brownie batter—it doesn't get any better than that. For easy clean-up, line the pan with foil before you add the batter; see how-to photos opposite.

active time 20 minutes *bake time* 25 to 30 minutes *makes* 24 brownies

¾ cup butter or margarine (1½ sticks)

4 squares (4 ounces) unsweetened chocolate

1 cup granulated sugar

1 cup packed light brown sugar

3 large eggs, lightly beaten

1 cup all-purpose flour

½ cup walnuts, coarsely chopped

1 teaspoon vanilla extract

½ teaspoon salt

1 cup individually wrapped caramels (25 to 30 caramels, depending on brand; see Tip), each cut in half

1 Preheat oven to 350°F. Line 13″ by 9″ baking pan with foil (see opposite).

2 In 3-quart saucepan, melt butter and chocolate over medium-low heat, stirring frequently. Remove saucepan from heat; stir in sugars and eggs until well mixed. Stir in flour, walnuts, vanilla, and salt just until blended.

3 Spread batter in prepared baking pan; sprinkle with caramels. Bake until toothpick inserted 2 inches from edge comes out almost clean, 25 to 30 minutes. Cool completely in pan on wire rack.

4 When cool, lift foil, with brownies, out of pan; peel foil away from sides. Cut lengthwise into 4 strips; then cut each strip crosswise into 6 pieces. (For easy slicing, dip the knife in warm water and wipe it clean before making each slice.) With small metal spatula, carefully remove brownies from pan.

5 Store brownies in cookie jar up to 3 days.

each brownie About 220 calories, 3g protein, 28g carbohydrate, 12g total fat (6g saturated fat), 1g fiber, 43mg cholesterol, 140mg sodium

brownie
tip

If you want the caramels to remain soft and gooey (our test kitchen's preference), buy a brand that lists sweetened condensed milk as its first ingredient. If you prefer the caramels to be firm and chewy, buy a brand that lists corn syrup or glucose first.

lining a pan with foil

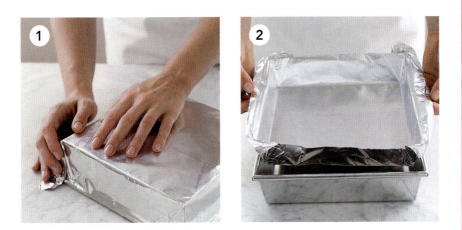

step 1: Turn the baking pan bottom side up. Cover the pan tightly with foil, shiny side out. Remove the foil cover.

step 2: Turn the baking pan right side up and carefully fit the molded foil into the pan, smoothing the foil to fit it into the edges.

Cocoa Brownies with Mini Chocolate Chips

The sprinkling of miniature chocolate chips on these rich brownies is a scrumptious addition. Be sure to cool these treats completely before serving or packing them, because they are sometimes just too soft to cut when warm.

active time 15 minutes plus cooling *bake time* 18 to 20 minutes *makes* 16 brownies

½ cup all-purpose flour
½ cup unsweetened cocoa
¼ teaspoon baking powder
¼ teaspoon salt
6 tablespoons butter or margarine
1 cup sugar
2 large eggs
2 teaspoons vanilla extract
⅓ cup mini chocolate chips

1 Preheat oven to 350°F. Line 8-inch square baking pan with foil (page 103); grease foil.

2 On waxed paper, combine flour, cocoa, baking powder, and salt.

3 In 3-quart saucepan, melt butter over low heat. Remove saucepan from heat; with rubber spatula, stir in sugar, then eggs, one a time, and vanilla until well blended. Stir in flour mixture.

4 Spread batter in prepared baking pan; sprinkle with chocolate chips. Bake until toothpick inserted 2 inches from center comes out almost clean, 18 to 20 minutes. Cool completely in pan on wire rack, 2 hours. When cool, lift foil, with brownie, out of pan; peel foil away from sides. Cut into 4 strips, then cut each strip crosswise into 4 squares.

5 Store brownies in cookie jar up to 3 days.

each brownie About 120 calories, 2g protein, 17g carbohydrate, 6g total fat (3g saturated fat), 1g fiber, 36mg cholesterol, 100mg sodium

Peanut Butter Swirl Brownies

The dark chocolate brownie offsets the nutty richness of the peanut butter.

active time 30 minutes plus cooling *bake time* 30 to 35 minutes *makes* 24 brownies

Brownie
- 1¼ cups all-purpose flour
- ¾ teaspoon baking powder
- ½ teaspoon salt
- ½ cup butter or margarine (1 stick)
- 4 squares (4 ounces) unsweetened chocolate
- 4 squares (4 ounces) semisweet chocolate
- 1½ cups sugar
- 2 teaspoons vanilla extract
- 4 large eggs, lightly beaten

Peanut Butter Swirl
- 1 cup creamy peanut butter
- ⅓ cup sugar
- 4 tablespoons butter or margarine
- 2 tablespoons all-purpose flour
- 1 teaspoon vanilla extract
- 1 large egg

1 Preheat oven to 350°F. Grease 13" by 9" baking pan.

2 Prepare brownie: On waxed paper, combine flour, baking powder, and salt. In 3-quart saucepan, melt butter and chocolates over low heat, stirring frequently. Remove saucepan from heat; stir in sugar. Add vanilla and eggs; stir until well mixed. Stir flour mixture into chocolate mixture until blended.

3 Prepare Peanut Butter Swirl: In medium bowl, with mixer on medium speed, beat peanut butter, sugar, butter, flour, vanilla, and egg until well blended.

4 Spread 2 cups chocolate batter in pan; top with peanut butter mixture arranged in 6 large dollops. Spoon remaining chocolate over and between peanut butter dollops. Use tip of knife to create swirled effect (see opposite).

5 Bake until toothpick inserted 2 inches from edge comes out almost clean, 30 to 35 minutes. Cool in pan on wire rack. When cool, cut lengthwise into 4 strips, then cut each strip crosswise into 6 pieces. With small metal spatula, carefully remove brownies from pan.

6 Store brownies in cookie jar up to 3 days.

each brownie About 265 calories, 6g protein, 26g carbohydrate, 17g total fat (8g saturated), 2g fiber, 61mg cholesterol, 185mg sodium

Marbling Brownie Batter

To produce a marbled effect with two different-colored batters, pull and swirl a kitchen knife through the batters as shown above.

Hazelnut Brownies

Toasting the nuts (see page 33) deepens their flavor.

active time 30 minutes *bake time* 25 to 30 minutes *makes* 24 brownies

1 cup all-purpose flour
½ teaspoon salt
¾ cup butter or margarine (1½ sticks)
4 squares (4 ounces) unsweetened chocolate
2 squares (2 ounces) semisweet chocolate
½ cup chocolate-hazelnut spread (about one-half 13-ounce jar)
1½ cups sugar
1 teaspoon vanilla extract
4 large eggs, lightly beaten
1 cup hazelnuts (filberts; 4 ounces), toasted (page 33) and coarsely chopped

1 Preheat oven to 350°F. Grease 13" by 9" baking pan.

2 In small bowl, with wire whisk, mix flour and salt.

3 In 3-quart saucepan, melt butter and chocolates over low heat, stirring frequently. Remove saucepan from heat; stir in hazelnut spread. Add sugar and vanilla; stir until well blended. Add eggs; stir until well mixed. Stir in flour mixture and hazelnuts just until blended.

4 Spread batter evenly in prepared baking pan. Bake until toothpick inserted 2 inches from edge comes out almost clean, 25 to 30 minutes. Cool in pan on wire rack. When cool, cut lengthwise into 4 strips, then cut each strip crosswise into 6 pieces. With small metal spatula, carefully remove brownies from pan.

5 Store brownies in cookie jar up to 3 days.

each brownie About 230 calories, 4g protein, 23g carbohydrate, 15g total fat (6g saturated), 2g fiber, 52mg cholesterol, 125mg sodium

cookie tip If you are mailing cookies, ship them early in the week so they don't sit in a warehouse over the weekend, and mark the box "FRAGILE AND PERISHABLE." And, of course, be sure to use enough crumpled newspaper, bubble wrap, or cellophane peanuts to cushion your goodies.

Cherry Linzer Bars

Christmas is the perfect time to rework this favorite treat as a delectable bar cookie.

active time 45 minutes   *bake time* 35 minutes plus cooling   *makes* 36 bars

½ cup dried tart cherries
2 tablespoons water
1¾ cups all-purpose flour
1 teaspoon ground cinnamon
½ teaspoon baking powder
¼ teaspoon salt
1 cup hazelnuts, toasted (page 33), skins rubbed off
½ cup granulated sugar
½ cup packed light brown sugar
¾ cup butter (1½ sticks), softened
½ teaspoon freshly grated lemon peel
1 large egg
1 jar (12 ounces) tart cherry jam confectioners' sugar, for garnish

1 Preheat oven to 350°F. In small bowl, combine cherries and water; microwave on High 1 minute. Set aside.

2 Meanwhile, line 13" by 9" baking pan with foil, with overhang at short ends. On waxed paper, combine flour, cinnamon, baking powder, and salt.

3 In food processor, pulse nuts and sugars until nuts are finely ground. Add butter and lemon peel; pulse until creamy. Blend in egg. Add flour mixture; pulse just until mixture comes together.

4 Reserve 1¼ cups dough; chill. With floured fingers, press remaining dough into bottom of prepared pan. Stir jam into cherries; spread over crust, up to ¼ inch from edges. With hands, roll chilled dough into ¼-inch-thick ropes; arrange diagonally, 1½ inches apart, over jam. Arrange remaining ropes around edge of pan. Bake 35 minutes or until dough is golden. Cool in pan on wire rack.

5 Transfer to cutting board. Cut into 36 bars. Store in airtight containers, layered with waxed paper, at room temperature up to 3 days or in freezer up to 1 month. Sprinkle with confectioners' sugar to serve.

each bar About 135 calories, 2g protein, 19g carbohydrate, 6g total fat (3g saturated), 1g fiber, 15mg cholesterol, 25mg sodium

Almond Lattice Brownies

These rich, grown-up brownies combine the deep, satisfying flavor of dark chocolate with the indulgence of almond paste.

active time 25 minutes plus cooling *bake time* 25 to 30 minutes *makes* 24 brownies

Brownies
- ½ cup butter or margarine (1 stick)
- 4 squares (4 ounces) unsweetened chocolate
- 4 squares (4 ounces) semisweet chocolate
- 1½ cups sugar
- 2 teaspoons vanilla extract
- 3 large eggs, lightly beaten
- 1¼ cups all-purpose flour
- ½ teaspoon salt

Almond Lattice Topping
- 1 tube or can (7 to 8 ounces) almond paste, crumbled
- 1 large egg
- ¼ cup sugar
- 1 tablespoon all-purpose flour
- 1 teaspoon vanilla extract

1 Preheat oven to 350°F. Grease 13" by 9" baking pan.

2 Prepare brownies: In 3-quart saucepan, melt butter and chocolates over medium-low heat, stirring frequently. Remove saucepan from heat; stir in sugar and vanilla. Add eggs; stir until well mixed. Stir in flour and salt just until blended. Spread batter in prepared baking pan.

3 Prepare topping: In food processor with knife blade attached, pulse almond paste, egg, sugar, flour, and vanilla until mixture is smooth. Transfer almond mixture to small zip-tight plastic bag. With scissors, cut bottom corner of bag diagonally ¼ inch from edge. Pipe almond topping over brownie batter to make 10 diagonal lines, each 1 inch apart. Pipe remaining topping, diagonally across first set of lines, to make 10 more lines and create a lattice pattern.

4 Bake until toothpick inserted 2 inches from edge comes out almost clean, 25 to 30 minutes. Cool in pan on wire rack. When cool, cut lengthwise into 4 strips, then cut each strip crosswise into 6 pieces. With small metal spatula, carefully remove brownies from pan.

5 Store brownies in cookie jar up to 3 days.

each brownie About 220 calories, 4g protein, 28g carbohydrate, 11g total fat (5g saturated), 2g fiber, 46mg cholesterol, 100mg sodium

Figgy Bars

Inspired by the famous figgy pudding loved by the Brits.

active time 25 minutes *bake time* 23 to 26 minutes *makes* 96 bars

Figgy Bars

- 10 ounces Black Mission figs, finely chopped
- 1 cup water
- 2 cups quick-cooking oats, uncooked
- 1½ cups packed brown sugar
- ⅔ cup dark molasses
- 6 tablespoons trans-fat free vegetable oil spread (60% to 70% oil)
- 2 large eggs
- 1 cup all-purpose flour
- 1 cup toasted wheat germ
- 2 teaspoons pumpkin-pie spice
- 2 teaspoons freshly grated orange peel
- 1 teaspoon salt
- 1 teaspoon baking soda
- 1 teaspoon baking powder
- 2 cups walnut halves

Hard Sauce Glaze

- 2 cups confectioners' sugar
- ¼ cup brandy
- 2 tablespoons warm water

1 Prepare Figgy Bars: Preheat oven to 350°F. Spray two 13" by 9" baking pans with nonstick cooking spray. Line pans with foil (page 103), extending foil 2 inches over short sides of pans; coat foil with spray.

2 In 4-quart saucepan, combine figs and water; heat to boiling over high heat. Remove saucepan from heat; stir in oats. Stir sugar, molasses, and vegetable oil spread into fig mixture until blended. Stir in eggs. Add flour, wheat germ, pumpkin-pie spice, orange peel, salt, baking soda, and baking powder, and stir until combined. Stir in walnuts. Divide batter equally between prepared pans; spread evenly.

3 Bake until toothpick inserted in center comes out clean, 23 to 26 minutes. Cool in pans on wire racks 10 minutes.

4 Meanwhile, prepare Hard Sauce Glaze: In small bowl, stir confectioners' sugar, brandy, and water until blended.

5 Remove bars from pans by lifting edges of foil; transfer on foil to racks. Brush hot pastries with glaze. Cool.

6 When cool, cut each lengthwise into 4 strips, then cut each strip crosswise into 6 rectangles. Cut each rectangle diagonally in half to make 96 triangles.

each bar About 75 calories, 4g protein, 12g carbohydrate, 2g total fat (0g saturated), 2g fiber, 4mg cholesterol, 50mg sodium

Chewy Ginger Triangles

Try these delightfully different bars if you're looking to change up your Christmas-cookie routine.

active time 20 minutes *bake time* 30 minutes *makes* 32 triangles

2 cups all-purpose flour

¾ cup butter or margarine (1½ sticks), softened

¾ cup sugar

½ cup (about 2 large rings) chopped candied pineapple

½ cup (about 2.7-ounce jar) chopped crystallized ginger (see Tip)

½ teaspoon salt

1 Preheat oven to 325°F. Into large bowl, measure all ingredients. With hands, knead ingredients until blended.

2 Pat dough into ungreased 13" by 9" baking pan. Bake until edges are golden, 30 minutes. Immediately cut lengthwise into 4 strips, then cut each strip crosswise into 4 pieces to form 16 bars. Cut each bar diagonally in half to form 32 triangles. Cool in pan on wire rack. With small metal spatula, carefully remove triangles from pan.

3 Store triangles in cookie jar up to 3 days.

each triangle About 100 calories, 1g protein, 15g carbohydrate, 4g total fat (0g saturated), 0g fiber, 0mg cholesterol, 90mg sodium

brownie tip

Crystallized ginger is ginger root that's been candied in a sugar syrup then tossed with granulated sugar. It's available in bags or sold in bulk at health-food stores and most supermarkets.

Granola Bars

Better than store-bought and super-simple to make—keep them on hand for an on-the-go energy boost during the busy Christmas season.

active time 15 minutes *bake time* 25 to 30 minutes *makes* 24 bars

2 cups old-fashioned oats, uncooked

1 cup all-purpose flour

1 cup chopped mixed dried fruit or dark seedless raisins

¾ cup packed light brown sugar

½ cup toasted wheat germ

¾ teaspoon ground cinnamon

¾ teaspoon salt

½ cup vegetable oil

½ cup pure maple syrup or maple-flavor syrup

2 teaspoons vanilla extract

1 large egg

1 Preheat oven to 350°F. Grease 13" by 9" baking pan. Line pan with foil (page 103); grease foil.

2 In large bowl, mix oats, flour, dried fruit, brown sugar, wheat germ, cinnamon, and salt until well combined. Stir in oil, syrup, vanilla, and egg until blended.

3 With wet hands, pat oat mixture into prepared pan. Bake until edges turn pale golden, 25 to 30 minutes. Cool completely in pan on wire rack. When cool, invert pan onto cutting board; remove foil. Cut lengthwise into 4 strips, then cut each strip crosswise into 6 pieces. With small metal spatula, carefully remove bars from pan.

4 Store bars in cookie jar up to 3 days.

each bar About 155 calories, 3g protein, 25g carbohydrate, 6g total fat (1g saturated), 2g fiber, 9mg cholesterol, 80mg sodium

Walnut Shortbread

Here's a shortbread with a delicate nutty flavor.

active time 20 minutes *bake time* 25 to 30 minutes *makes* 24 cookies

½ cup walnuts, toasted
(page 33)
1½ cups all-purpose flour
½ cup sugar
½ cup butter or margarine
(1 stick), softened

1 Preheat oven to 325°F. In food processor with knife blade attached, process walnuts with ½ cup flour until nuts are finely ground.

2 In medium bowl, combine remaining 1 cup flour, the sugar, and walnut mixture until blended. With fingertips, blend butter into walnut mixture until well combined and crumbly.

3 With hands, press dough onto bottom of ungreased 9-inch square baking pan. Bake until light golden, 25 to 30 minutes. While still warm, cut into 4 strips, then cut each strip crosswise into 6 pieces. Cool completely in pan on wire rack. With small metal spatula, carefully remove shortbread from pan.

4 Store in cookie jar up to 1 week.

each bar About 95 calories, 1g protein, 11g carbohydrate, 5g total fat (3g saturated), 0g fiber, 10mg cholesterol, 39mg sodium

cookie tip

If you press bar cookies gently into granulated sugar before placing them in a jar or tin, they will be far less likely to stick to one another.

Shapely Shortbread

Shortbread is sometimes formed using a mold that shapes the dough and creates raised patterns on its surface. The dough is packed into the mold, which looks like a thick ceramic or wooden plate with flutings and designs carved deeply into its inner surface. Since shortbread is a Scottish specialty, you'll often see these attractive molds decorated with a thistle, which is the national emblem of Scotland.

Lemon-Cranberry Shortbread

These glazed bars are especially festive for the holidays.

active time 30 minutes plus standing *bake time* 35 to 40 minutes *makes* 36 bars

2 to 3 lemons
¾ cup cold butter (1½ sticks), cut into pieces (do not use margarine)
¼ cup granulated sugar
1½ cups confectioners' sugar
2 cups all-purpose flour
½ cup dried cranberries

1 Preheat oven to 300°F. Line 13" by 9" baking pan with foil (page 103).

2 From lemons, grate 2 tablespoons plus ½ teaspoon peel and squeeze 2 tablespoons plus 1 teaspoon juice.

3 In food processor with knife blade attached, process butter, granulated sugar, ½ cup confectioners' sugar, 2 tablespoons lemon peel, and 1 tablespoon lemon juice until creamy. Add flour and pulse until dough begins to come together. Add cranberries and pulse until evenly mixed into dough.

4 Press dough evenly onto bottom of prepared baking pan. Bake until edges are lightly browned and top is pale golden, 35 to 40 minutes. Cool in pan on wire rack.

5 Combine remaining 1 cup confectioners' sugar, 1 tablespoon lemon juice, and remaining ½ teaspoon lemon peel until smooth. Add more juice to reach a good spreading consistency as needed. Spread glaze evenly over cooled shortbread. Let stand 30 minutes. When glaze has set, lift foil, with shortbread, out of pan; peel foil away from sides. Cut lengthwise into 3 strips, then cut each strip crosswise into 12 bars.

6 Store in cookie jar up to 4 days.

each bar About 90 calories, 1g protein, 13g carbohydrate, 4g total fat (3g saturated), 0.5g fiber, 11mg cholesterol, 40mg sodium

Tin Roof Puffed Rice Treats

These nostalgic cereal treats celebrate the sweet-salty combination featured in tin roof sundaes, a chocolate sundae topped with red-skinned Spanish peanuts that was popular in the early twentieth century.

active time 20 minutes plus chilling *makes* 16 treats

½ cup creamy peanut butter

24 large marshmallows

4 cups puffed rice cereal

4 ounces semisweet chocolate chips (⅔ cup)

2 tablespoons roasted, salted Spanish peanuts, chopped

1 Spray 8-inch square baking pan with nonstick cooking spray.

2 In microwave-safe 4-quart bowl, combine peanut butter and marshmallows. Cover bowl with vented plastic wrap and cook in microwave on High 1 minute, until melted. With rubber spatula, quickly stir in puffed rice until evenly coated. With hand, evenly pat puffed rice mixture into prepared baking pan.

3 In microwave-safe cup, heat chocolate in microwave on High 35 to 45 seconds, or until soft; stir until smooth. With offset spatula, spread melted chocolate on top of puffed rice mixture. Sprinkle with peanuts; gently press so nuts adhere to chocolate.

4 Refrigerate until chocolate is set, 30 minutes. Cut lengthwise into 4 strips, then cut each strip crosswise into 4 pieces. With small metal spatula, remove treats from pan.

5 Store treats in cookie jar up to 3 days.

each treat About 135 calories, 3g protein, 18g carbohydrate, 7g total fat (2g saturated), 1g fiber, 0mg cholesterol, 51mg sodium

Metric Equivalents

The recipes in this book use the standard United States method for measuring liquid and dry or solid ingredients (teaspoons, tablespoons, and cups). The information on this chart is provided to help cooks outside the U.S. successfully use these recipes. All equivalents are approximate.

Metric Equivalents for Different Types of Ingredients

A standard cup measure of a dry or solid ingredient will vary in weight depending on the type of ingredient. A standard cup of liquid is the same volume for any type of liquid. Use the following chart when converting standard cup measures to grams (weight) or milliliters (volume).

Standard Cup	Fine Powder (e.g., flour)	Grain (e.g., rice)	Granular (e.g., sugar)	Liquid Solids (e.g., butter)	Liquid (e.g., milk)
1	140 g	150 g	190 g	200 g	240 ml
¾	105 g	113 g	143 g	150 g	180 ml
⅔	93 g	100 g	125 g	133 g	160 ml
½	70 g	75 g	95 g	100 g	120 ml
⅓	47 g	50 g	63 g	67 g	80 ml
¼	35 g	38 g	48 g	50 g	60 ml
⅛	18 g	19 g	24 g	25 g	30 ml

Useful Equivalents for Liquid Ingredients by Volume

¼ tsp =				1 ml
½ tsp =				2 ml
1 tsp =				5 ml
3 tsp =	1 tblsp =		½ fl oz =	15 ml
	2 tblsp =	⅛ cup =	1 fl oz =	30 ml
	4 tblsp =	¼ cup =	2 fl oz =	60 ml
	5 ⅓ tblsp =	⅓ cup =	3 fl oz =	80 ml
	8 tblsp =	½ cup =	4 fl oz =	120 ml
	10 ⅔ tblsp =	⅔ cup =	5 fl oz =	160 ml
	12 tblsp =	¾ cup =	6 fl oz =	180 ml
	16 tblsp =	1 cup =	8 fl oz =	240 ml
	1 pt =	2 cups =	16 fl oz =	480 ml
	1 qt =	4 cups =	32 fl oz =	960 ml
			33 fl oz =	1000 ml 1 L

Useful Equivalents for Dry Ingredients by Weight

(To convert ounces to grams, multiply the number of ounces by 30.)

1 oz =	1/16 lb =	30 g
4 oz =	1/4 lb =	120 g
8 oz =	1/2 lb =	240 g
12 oz =	3/4 lb =	360 g
16 oz =	1 lb =	480 g

Useful Equivalents for Cooking/Oven Temperatures

	Farenheit	Celcius	Gas Mark
Freeze Water	32°F	0°C	
Room Temperature	68°F	20°C	
Boil Water	212°F	100°C	
Bake	325°F	160°C	3
	350°F	180°C	4
	375°F	190°C	5
	400°F	200°C	6
	425°F	220°C	7
	450°F	230°C	8
Broil			Grill

Index

Anise Slices, 97
Applesauce-Raisin Cookies with Lemon Glaze, 38–39
Apricots
    Apricot Fudgies, 42–43
    Apricot Oatmeal Cookies, 32

Baking powder, 9
Baking soda, 9
Baking tips
    for brownies and bar cookies, 100
    chocolate types and tips, 11–12
    cookie sheet selection and use, 14–15
    cooling cookies, 15
    for drop cookies, 18
    for icebox cookies, 82
    ingredients, 8–9
    measuring equipment and tips, 12–13
    mixing ingredients, 14
    for shaped cookies, 52
    timing, 15
Basic Cookie Dough, 84
Biscotti. *See also* Mandelbrot
    Cherry and Ginger Biscotti, 76–77
    Crunchy Low-Fat Chocolate Biscotti, 78–79
    Triple-Nut Biscotti, 74, 75
Brownies and bar cookies, 99–121
    about: baking tips, 100; marbling batter, 107; overview of, 99

Almond Lattice Brownies, 112, 113
Almond Thins, 101
Caramel-Nut Brownies, 102–103
Cherry Linzer Bars, 110
Chewy Ginger Triangles, 115
Cocoa Brownies with Mini Chocolate Chips, 104–105
Figgy Bars, 114
Granola Bars, 116–117
Hazelnut Brownies, 108, 109
Lemon-Cranberry Shortbread, 120
Peanut Butter Swirl Brownies, 98, 106–107
Tin Roof Puffed Rice Treats, 121
Walnut Shortbread, 118–119
Brown Sugar Pecan Crisps, 26
Butter, 8, 13
Butterscotch Fingers, 88, 89

Caramel-Nut Brownies, 102–103
Checkerboard Cookies, 94–95
Cherries
    Cherry and Ginger Biscotti, 76–77
    Cherry Linzer Bars, 110
    Oatmeal-Chocolate-Cherry Cookies, 34, 35
Chocolate. *See also* Brownies and bar cookies
    about: bittersweet, 11; chips, 12; cocoa powder, 11; melting, 12; quality of, 11; semisweet, 11; storing, 12; sweet, 11; types of, 11–12; unsweetened, 11; white, 12
    Apricot Fudgies, 42–43
    Checkerboard Cookies, 94–95
    Chipperdoodles, 60
    Chocolate Chip Cookies, 20, 21
    Chocolate Chunk Cookies, 19
    Chocolate Crinkles, 54–55
    Chocolate-Hazelnut Macaroons, 48, 49
    Chocolate Pinwheels, 93
    Chocolate Sambuca Cookies, 56
    Chocolate Wows, 16, 44–45
    Cranberry-Chocolate Chunk Cookies, 40
    Crunchy Low-Fat Chocolate Biscotti, 78–79
    Healthy Makeover Chocolate-Chip Oatmeal Cookies, 30–31
    Mint Brownie Bites, 53
    Oatmeal-Chocolate-Cherry Cookies, 34, 35
    Triple-Chocolate Chubbies, 46
    White Chocolate-Peppermint Chippers, 41
Cocoa powder. *See also* Chocolate
Coconut
    Coconut Macaroons, 47
    Coconut-Oatmeal Crisps, 29
Cookie sheets, 14–15, 100

Cooling cookies, 15
Cranberries
    Cranberry-Chocolate
        Chunk Cookies, 40
    Cranberry-Orange Spice
        Cookies, 96
    Lemon-Cranberry
        Shortbread, 120
Crosshatch marks, 22

Drop cookies, 17–49
    about: baking tips, 18;
        making crosshatch
        marks, 22; overview of, 17
    Applesauce-Raisin
        Cookies with Lemon
        Glaze, 38–39
    Apricot Fudgies, 42–43
    Apricot Oatmeal Cookies,
        32
    Brown Sugar Pecan
        Crisps, 26
    Chewy Molasses Spice
        Cookies, 20, 24
    Chocolate Chip Cookies,
        20, 21
    Chocolate Chunk
        Cookies, 19
    Chocolate-Hazelnut
        Macaroons, 48, 49
    Chocolate Wows, 16,
        44–45
    Classic Oatmeal-Raisin
        Cookies, 28
    Coconut Macaroons, 47
    Coconut-Oatmeal
        Crisps, 29
    Cranberry-Chocolate
        Chunk Cookies, 40
    Ginger Cookies, 25
    Healthy Makeover
        Chocolate-Chip
        Oatmeal Cookies,
        30–31

Oatmeal-Chocolate-
    Cherry Cookies, 34, 35
Peanut Butter Cookies,
    20, 22–23
Sour-Cream Cookies, 27
Thumbprint Jammies,
    36–37
Triple-Chocolate
    Chubbies, 46
White Chocolate-
    Peppermint Chippers,
    41

Figgy Bars, 114
Flour
    measuring, 13
    types of, 9
Foil, lining pans with, 103
Freezing dough, 82

Ginger
    Cherry and Ginger
        Biscotti, 76–77
    Chewy Ginger Triangles,
        115
    Ginger Cookies, 25
    Gingerbread Cutouts, 87
    Whole-Grain
        Gingersnaps, 61
Granola Bars, 116–117
Greasing cookie sheets, 15

Hermits, 68, 69
Honey Cookies, 66
Honey, measuring, 13

Icebox cookies, 81–97
    about: baking tips,
        82; forming/slicing
        checkerboard dough,
        95; overview of, 81;
        shaping and slicing, 85
    Almond Slices, 92
    Anise Slices, 97

Basic Cookie Dough, 84
Butterscotch Fingers, 88, 89
Checkerboard Cookies,
    94–95
Chocolate Pinwheels, 93
Cranberry-Orange Spice
    Cookies, 96
Garden-Party Sugar
    Cookies, 83
Gingerbread Cutouts, 87
Lime Slice-'n'-Bakes, 86
Maple Pecan Cookies, 90
Oatmeal Icebox Cookies, 91
Ingredients, 8–9. See also
    specific ingredients

Jams and jellies
    Best Linzer Cookies, 70
    Thumbprint Jammies,
        36–37

Lemons
    about: juicing, 39
    Lemon-Cranberry
        Shortbread, 120
    Lemon Glaze, 38–39
Lime Slice-'n'-Bakes, 86
Liquids, measuring, 13

Mandelbrot, 72–73
Maple Pecan Cookies, 90
Maple syrup, measuring, 13
Marbling batter, 107
Margarine, 8, 13
Measuring, equipment and
    tips, 12–13, 122–123
Melt-Aways, 57
Metric equivalents,
    122–123
Mint Brownie Bites, 53
Mixing tips, 14
Molasses
    Chewy Molasses Spice
        Cookies, 20

Molasses Cookies, 62

Nuts. *See also* Peanut
 butter
 about: skinning hazelnuts,
 33; toasting, 33
 Almond Lattice
 Brownies, 112, 113
 Almond Slices, 92
 Almond Thins, 101
 Brown Sugar Pecan
 Crisps, 26
 Butterscotch Fingers, 88,
 89
 Caramel-Nut Brownies,
 102–103
 Chocolate-Hazelnut
 Macaroons, 48, 49
 Hazelnut Brownies, 108,
 109
 Mandelbrot, 72–73
 Maple Pecan Cookies, 90
 Triple-Nut Biscotti, 74, 75
 Walnut Balls, 64–65
 Walnut Shortbread,
 118–119
 Wheat-Free Almond
 Butter Cookies, 67

Oatmeal
 Classic Oatmeal-Raisin
 Cookies, 28
 Coconut-Oatmeal
 Crisps, 29
 Granola Bars, 116–117
 Healthy Makeover
 Chocolate-Chip
 Oatmeal Cookies,
 30–31
 Oatmeal-Chocolate-
 Cherry Cookies, 34, 35
 Oatmeal Icebox Cookies, 91

Pans
 for brownies and bar
 cookies, 100
 cookie sheets, 14–15
 lining with foil, 103
Peanut butter
 Peanut Butter Cookies,
 20, 22–23
 Peanut Butter Swirl
 Brownies, 98,
 106–107

Raisins
 Applesauce-Raisin
 Cookies with Lemon
 Glaze, 38–39
 Classic Oatmeal-Raisin
 Cookies, 28
Rice, in Tin Roof Puffed
 Rice Treats, 121

Shaped cookies, 75–79.
 See also Biscotti
 about: baking tips, 52;
 overview of, 75
 Best Linzer Cookies, 70
 Chipperdoodles, 60
 Chocolate Crinkles, 54–55
 Chocolate Sambuca
 Cookies, 56
 Hermits, 68, 69
 Honey Cookies, 66
 Mandelbrot, 72–73
 Melt-Aways, 57
 Melt-in-Your-Mouth
 Sugar Cookies, 63
 Mint Brownie Bites, 53
 Molasses Cookies, 62
 Snickerdoodles, 58, 59
 Walnut Balls, 64–65
 Wheat-Free Almond
 Butter Cookies, 67

Whole-Grain Gingersnaps,
 61
Shortbread, 118–120
Skinning hazelnuts, 33
Snickerdoodles, 58, 59
Sour-Cream Cookies, 27
Spice cookies
 Chewy Molasses Spice
 Cookies, 20, 24
 Cranberry-Orange Spice
 Cookies, 96
 Hermits, 68, 69
Sugar cookies
 Brown Sugar Pecan
 Crisps, 26
 Garden-Party Sugar
 Cookies, 83
 Melt-in-Your-Mouth
 Sugar Cookies, 63
 Snickerdoodles, 58, 59
 Sugar, measuring, 13

Thumbprint Jammies,
 36–37
Timing tips, 15
Tin Roof Puffed Rice
 Treats, 121
Toasting nuts, 33

Washing cookie sheets, 15
Wheat-Free Almond Butter
 Cookies, 67
White chocolate. *See*
 Chocolate

Photography Credits

Monica Buck: 61, 74
Tara Donne: 31
Brian Hagiwara: 13, 43
Getty Images: Dennis Gottlieb, 79; Alison Miksch, 119; Paul Viant, 10
iStockphoto: Donald Erickson, 47, 62; Ekaterina Fribus, 55; Christine Glade, 14;
    Bryce Kroll, 8; Wojtek Kryczka, 11; Bill Noll, 15; John Sigler, 27
Frances Janisch: 20, 22, 34, 65
Yunhee Kim: 16, 98, 111
Rita Maas: 6, 33, 108, 112, 120
Kate Mathis: 80, 87, 105, 117
Ellie Miller: 93, 96
Steven Mark Needham: 48, 73, 85
Kate Sears: 50, 53, 70
Stockfood: Paul Poplis, 58; Anthony-Masterson, 77; Photo Op, 83
Ann Stratton: 19, 28, 36, 37, 39, 68, 88, 89
Studio D: Philip Friedman, 7
Mark Thomas: 2, 23, 44, 45, 95, 103, 107, 128

Cover
Front: Kate Sears
Inside front: Mark Thomas
Back: Paul Poplis/Stockfood (upper right); Kate Mathis (upper left); Ekaterina Fribus/
    iStock (lower right); Rita Maas (lower left)

Recipe Cards
for You to Share

As a bonus, we've included thirty-two blank recipe cards. The perforated rules make them easy to remove. Simply fill in a favorite cookie recipe, tear out the card, and deliver it to friends or family—along with a batch of freshly baked cookies!

Recipe For ✳ _____

Recipe For ✳ _____

Recipe For ✳ _____

Recipe For ✳ _____

Recipe For ✳

Recipe For ✳

Recipe For ✳

Recipe For ✳

Recipe For ✳

Recipe For ✳

Recipe For ✳

Recipe For ✳

Recipe For ✳

Recipe For ✳

Recipe For ✳

Recipe For ✳

Recipe For ✳ _____

Recipe For ✳ _____

Recipe For ✳ _____

Recipe For ✳ _____

Recipe For ✳

Recipe For ✳

Recipe For ✳

Recipe For ✳

Recipe For ✳ _____

Recipe For ✳ _____

Recipe For ✳ _____

Recipe For ✳ _____

Recipe For ✳ _____

Recipe For ✳ _____

Recipe For ✳ _____

Recipe For ✳ _____